W9-BNE-814

WORDS THAT CHANGED THE WORLD

UNDERSTANDING
RACHEL CARSON'S
SILENT SPRING

ALEX MACGILLIVRAY

ROSEN
PUBLISHING®

New York

This edition published in 2011 by:

The Rosen Publishing Group, Inc.
29 East 21st Street
New York, NY 10010

Additional end matter copyright © 2011 by The Rosen Publishing Group, Inc.

Library of Congress Cataloging-in-Publication Data

MacGillivray, Alex.
Understanding Rachel Carson's *Silent Spring* / Alex MacGillivray.
    p. cm.—(Words that changed the world)
Includes bibliographical references and index.
ISBN 978-1-4488-1670-5 (library binding)
1. Carson, Rachel, 1907–1964. Silent spring. 2. Pesticides—Environmental aspects. 3. Pesticides—Toxicology.
4. Pesticides and wildlife. 5. Insect pests—Biological control. I. Title.
QH545.P4C3837 2010
363.738'498—dc22

                                                                                    2010009260

Manufactured in the United States of America

CPSIA Compliance Information: Batch #S10YA: For further information, contact Rosen Publishing, New York, New York, at 1-800-237-9932.

Text and design copyright © 2004 by The Ivy Press. This edition of *Manifesto: Rachel Carson's Silent Spring* originally published in 2004 is published by arrangement with The Ivy Press Limited. From *Silent Spring* by Rachel Carson, Copyright © 1962 by Rachel L. Carson, renewed by Roger Christie. Reprinted by permission of Houghton Mifflin Company. All rights reserved.

Picture credits
The author and publisher are grateful to the following for permission to reproduce illustrations:

Corbis: 20, 27 Kevin Fleming, 34B David H. Wells, 45 Genevive Naylor, 49 Gary W. Carter, 62 Charles E. Rotkin, 70 Jonathan Blair, 72, 79
        Hulton-Deutsch, 91 Wally McNamee, 105 Jonathan Blair, 115 Kapoor Baldev/Sygma, 118 Pallava Bagla.
Corbis /Bettmann Archive: 8, 9, 14, 21, 28, 31, 37, 38, 41, 54, 64, 65, 71, 76, 77, 85, 89R, 90, 95, 97, 122R.
Courtesy of the Lear/Carson Collection: 23T, 68.
Library of Congress/Prints and Photographs Division: 12, 19, 29, 82.
The National Oceanic Atmospheric Administration: 25.
U.S. Department of Agriculture/Agriculture Research Service/Photos by Scott Bauer: 16, 34T, 36, 100T, 102, 117.
USDA/Keith Weller: 100B.
U.S. Fish and Wildlife Service: 10 George Nelson, 15 Aaron D. Drew, 33 Rex Gary Schmidt, 52 Dave Menke, 81 Alaska Image Library, 89L
        David Hall, 122R Karen Bollington.
Yale Collection of American Literature, Beinecke Rare Book and Manuscript Library: 7 Brooks and Co. Studio, 23B, 24 Edwin Gray, 26 & 48 &
        58 Courtesy Rachel Carson Estate, 67, 99, 121.

CONTENTS

UNDERSTANDING RACHEL CARSON'S *SILENT SPRING*
INTRODUCTION

Silent Spring is the green manifesto that made ecology a household name, and pesticides a dirty word. It has been read by millions and has influenced two generations of environmental activists. Derived from the Italian "to make evident," a manifesto clearly explains problems and solutions for a broad audience. The timely brilliance of the thought and writing give a manifesto an impact beyond all proportion to its word count. Only a handful of books have had such an impact, and by general consent, *Silent Spring* was the first—and remains the only—manifesto on environmental issues.

Silent Spring is a strange hybrid from an era when science writing and literature were separate genres addressing different audiences. Its prose is lyrical, yet the opening "Fable for Tomorrow" is terrifying. Behind its passionate ecology lies a body of complex scientific evidence that only a gifted writer could explain to a general audience. Because of pesticides, the book warned, "early mornings are strangely silent where once they were filled with the beauty of bird song," but its impact came as much from fear of cancer as from threats to wildlife. In the popular consciousness, the idea of a Silent Spring was as frightening as an atomic mushroom cloud.

> *She wrote a revolutionary book in terms that were acceptable to a middle class emerging from the lethargy of post-war affluence.*
>
> Linda Lear, Rachel Carson's biographer

Rachel Carson (1907–1964), the author of *Silent Spring*, is also a paradox: a best-selling author who was initially reluctant to write about pesticides. She was an intensely private person who became a major public figure and—after her death less than two years after publication—an icon for ecologists and feminists. She confronted a "Neanderthal," male-dominated chemical industry with appeals to ordinary American women. The industry counterattack was swift and ruthless, but in April 1998, *Time* magazine voted her into its list of Top 100 people of the twentieth century, and DDT, the pesticide she campaigned against, was voted one of the 100 worst ideas of the century.

Unlike some manifestos, *Silent Spring*'s impact was powerful and immediate, catching President John F. Kennedy's attention in the thick of the Cold War. It led rapidly to government inquiries, court cases, popular protests, the creation of the Environmental Protection Agency, and the banning of the worst pesticides. The book was midwife at the birth of a worldwide environmental movement in the early 1970s.

Rachel Carson was a meticulous writer who sometimes wrote just a few hundred words in a day. Carson would read her work aloud and make frequent revisions.

As a symbol of the book's ecological impact, the bald eagle has returned from the brink of extinction. Yet almost five decades later, dangers still threaten the "web of life" that *Silent Spring* first introduced to the public. From global warming to genetic modification, big business and its supporters continue to deny evidence of harm with the vehemence that so infuriated Carson. Even DDT has persistent advocates, and is still used in the world's two most populous countries, India and China.

Rachel Carson only reluctantly set out to write a manifesto—but *Silent Spring* became the most readable and enduring environmental crusading book ever written, still selling more than 60 copies a day. Despite its enormous impact nearly 50 years, the problems it brought to light are still far from solved.

UNDERSTANDING
RACHEL CARSON'S *SILENT SPRING*
CONTEXT
AND CREATOR

Carson was particularly incensed by aerial spraying. "Although today's poisons are more dangerous than any known before," she wrote, "they have amazingly become something to be showered down indiscriminately from the skies."

Collision Course: Chemists and Ecologists

Around the time of World War II, European industrial chemists found uses for a group of hitherto obscure chemical substances that would come to be seen as "the perfect pesticides." In Europe during the war, these chemicals were sometimes designed to take human life (as nerve poisons), and sometimes to save it (by combating insect-borne disease). And after the war ended, these powerfully toxic substances were enthusiastically applied in the United States, on a massive scale, to control agricultural pests.

Throughout the 1950s, evidence was emerging of alarming declines in the populations of American birds, from the beloved robin to the magnificent bald eagle. This was noted by tens of thousands of ordinary Americans—including Carson—who were passionate bird-watchers. The "perfect pesticides" had become the darlings of the chemical industry, but were they responsible for this decline? A clash between the chemists and the ecologists was inevitable. And it was Rachel Carson's book, *Silent Spring*, that proved to be the catalyst for the formation of a mainstream environmental consciousness. In effect, *Silent Spring* was the first green manifesto.

Early Ecologists: From Celebration to Conservation

Although ecology as a science developed first in Europe, its strength as a popular movement began in the United States. The vast American wilderness had no parallel in western Europe, nor did the speed and scale at which the industrialization of agriculture took place. In response to assaults on the magnificent natural environment, the "nature study movement," as it was known in the early days, began its transformation into a campaigning ecological movement, merging literary enterprise and scientific investigation with practical conservation activity and political lobbying.

Ecology as we know it today owes a great deal to the English naturalist Charles Darwin's pioneering work on natural selection. His celebration of the diversity and interdependence of species and their habitats, particularly in *On the Origin of Species* (1859), set the stage for a new understanding of the natural world. The term *ecology* was coined in the 1890s by the German zoologist-philosopher Ernst Haeckel (1834–1919), an early exponent of Darwin's theories. However, for many decades afterward, only a small coterie of scientists used this technical term to understand the distribution and abundance of species.

During the 1850s, American writers such as Henry David Thoreau in *Walden* (1854) and Walt Whitman with *Leaves of Grass* (1855) were celebrating a lyrical strand of American environmentalism, planting the literary seeds of the movement. However, by the end of the century, literary naturalists were gradually moving away from a spirit of celebration to one of consternation—in reaction to damage to the environment caused by intensive logging, mining, and railroad construction.

Popular concern was also growing. In 1886 George Bird Grinnell, editor of the journal *Forest and Stream*, invited readers to sign a pledge against harming any bird. So many

Charles Darwin (1809–1882) was the British scientist who developed the theory of evolution through natural selection. Darwin, here in a watercolor by George Richmond, first published *On the Origin of Species* in 1859. Unlike Rachel Carson, he lived long enough to revise his masterpiece repeatedly.

An early naturalist and feathered friend on Florida's Pelican Island. This was the first National Wildlife Refuge in the United States, set up in 1903. Within two years, nature warden Guy Bradley had been murdered by poachers.

people responded—almost 40,000—that Grinnell could not cope with the numbers. This was the start of the group known as the Audubon Society for the Protection of Birds. In response to such popular sentiment, the federal government began a modest process in the 1860s and 1870s of conserving a few areas of outstanding natural beauty, such as Yellowstone (1872), as national parks. A National Park Service was also set up to manage the slow growth of a network created by sporadic acts of Congress.

In 1891 Congress granted the president powers to reserve forestland. President Benjamin Harrison promptly reserved 13 million acres (52, 609 square km), and Grover Cleveland in his second term in office (1893–1897) doubled that area. But it was Theodore Roosevelt, personally committed to conservation, who really got the system going during his term in office between 1901 and 1909, bringing national forests up to 194 million acres (785, 090 sq km). (In 2001 the outgoing president, Bill Clinton, tried to rival this with measures to protect 60 million acres (242,811 sq km) of wild national forests.) Roosevelt strengthened the conservation focus of the Division of Forestry (now the Forest Service) under Gifford Pinchot (1865–1946), who had studied forestry in Europe. Roosevelt is also credited with setting up the first National Wildlife Refuge—Florida's Pelican Island—in 1903.

What Roosevelt meant by the term *conservation* became clear in a weeklong White House conference on the subject in 1908. Conservation did not in fact mean the preservation of intact wilderness. Rather, it was a utilitarian concept of the optimal management of natural resources for the greatest good of the greatest number of people. "Forest protection is not an end in itself," said Roosevelt. "It is a means to increase and sustain the resources of our country and the industries which depend upon them. The preservation of our forests is an imperative business necessity."

Writers and Activists:
The Birth of a Conservation Movement

According to Robert E. Taylor, who discussed the birth of the modern environmental movement in his book *Ahead of the Curve* (1990), the main challenge to Roosevelt's vision of conservation came from the keen outdoorsman John Muir. Muir, a founder of the Sierra Club, which was set up in 1892 to promote the conservation of the Sierra Nevada, helped to forge a rival conservation ethic from growing demands for the protection of wildlife and wilderness. Initially progress was slow: Muir founded the Sierra Club in 1892, but by 1903 it had attracted a grand total of only 663 members.

Everybody needs beauty as well as bread, places to play in and pray in where nature may heal and give strength to body and soul alike.

John Muir, Yosemite, 1912

Tensions arose, however, as the Sierra Club, like the newly incorporated National Association of Audubon Societies, began to attract more and more active members. Muir used to go hiking with government forester Gifford Pinchot, but the two fell out bitterly over plans to flood the Tuolumne River in Hetch-Hetchy Valley,

HETCH HETCHY RESERVOIR SITE

HEARING

BEFORE THE

COMMITTEE ON PUBLIC LANDS
UNITED STATES SENATE

SIXTY-THIRD CONGRESS
FIRST SESSION

ON

H. R. 7207

AN ACT GRANTING TO THE CITY AND COUNTY OF SAN FRANCISCO,
CERTAIN RIGHTS OF WAY IN, OVER, AND THROUGH CERTAIN
PUBLIC LANDS, THE YOSEMITE NATIONAL PARK, AND
STANISLAUS NATIONAL FOREST, AND CERTAIN LANDS
IN THE YOSEMITE NATIONAL PARK, THE STANIS-
LAUS NATIONAL FOREST, AND THE PUBLIC
LANDS IN THE STATE OF CALIFORNIA,
AND FOR OTHER PURPOSES

[Printed for the use of the Committee on Public Lands]

WASHINGTON
GOVERNMENT PRINTING OFFICE
1913

The proposal to build a reservoir in the scenic Hetch-Hetchy Valley outraged the early conservation movement in the first decade of the twentieth century. Despite public hearings and protests, the government gave the scheme the go-ahead, and the valley was flooded in 1913.

California, to provide water for a rapidly growing San Francisco. Growing conflicts over the use of natural resources between conservationists, government, and business came to a head when poachers murdered pioneer nature warden Guy Bradley in 1905. Conservationists lost the battle to protect the Hetch-Hetchy, which was flooded in 1913. In that symbolic year, the very last passenger pigeon, Martha, died in a zoo.

In the 1930s the New Deal—a package of domestic works programs designed to tackle the economic depression—saw unprecedented damming and forestry activity, and corresponding growth in the conservation movement. By 1930, the Sierra Club had more than 2,500 members, and in 1934 came the publication of Roger Tory Peterson's *A Field Guide to the Birds*. This, according to the National Audubon Society, "popularized birding as never before."

During this period, which saw a slowly growing environmental consciousness, a number of writers began to experiment with a new genre blending science with literature. British author Henry Williamson penned two classics of the genre, *Tarka the Otter* (1927) and *Salar the Salmon* (1935), much admired by Rachel Carson. She also respected Henry Beston's nature writing, particularly *The Outermost House* (1924), and Ada Govan's later memoir *Wings at My Window* (1940). Aldo Leopold's nature writing, published posthumously as *A Sand County Almanac* (1949), continued this new literary genre, which remains popular today.

Such was the state of the small but energetic ecological movement in the United States on the eve of World War II. It was influenced by the growing science of ecology, by a literary genre, and by practical activities in defense of natural areas of beauty and America's diversity of animal life. But as Rachel Carson knew only too well from her work in the Fish and Wildlife Service and her involvement in Audubon, the movement was fragile. Knowledge and understanding of the science, the literature, and the nascent campaigns had not yet reached Main Street. "Ecology" was far from being a household word.

The Chemistry Set: Inventing Perfect Poisons

Alfred Nobel invented dynamite in 1866 and built up companies and laboratories in more than 20 countries all over the world. A holder of more than 350 patents, he also wrote poetry and drama and seriously considered becoming a writer. With an irony of which he was only too well aware, he was prescribed for his heart condition the very nitroglycerin he had used for more destructive purposes (Rachel Carson would also be prescribed this high explosive for angina as her health deteriorated in the early 1960s).

Nobel facilitated mass destruction, but he was also an armchair ecologist. In his library—in between the collected works of Victor Hugo, tracts on peace, technical

I have examined Man's wonderful inventions. And I tell you that in the arts of life Man invents nothing; but in the arts of death he outdoes Nature herself, and produces by chemistry and machinery all the slaughter of plague, pestilence, and famine.

The Devil in *Don Juan in Hell*, George Bernard Shaw, 1902

Swiss chemist Paul Müller discovered that the chemical DDT was a potent pesticide. Indeed, it helped save lives in World War II. Müller won the Nobel Prize in 1948, but problems with the pesticide soon emerged.

handbooks on torpedoes, and guides to U.S. patent law—are books by Darwin and Haeckel, the pioneers of ecology. Today he is remembered more for the prizes he set up— especially the Peace Prize.

The Nobel Prize-winning career of Swiss industrial chemist Paul Hermann Müller (1899–1965) displays similar ironies. He and Carson were contemporaries: he was born eight years before her and outlived her by just a year. They never met, and Müller merits just one brief mention in *Silent Spring*. Yet Müller's scientific research led directly to Carson's writing *Silent Spring*. He was the first person to discover the efficiency as a pesticide of a long-forgotten chemical compound called dichlorodiphenyltrichloroethane (DDT). Unlike many newly discovered chemicals in the 1930s and 1940s, DDT found humanitarian applications during World War II, notably preventing an outbreak of typhoid in Naples, Italy. But its benefits were soon outweighed by the damage it inflicted on the environment—and people—in the following decades.

In 1774 the Swedish apothecary Karl Wilhelm Scheele had detected the element chlorine. This discovery marked the inauguration of a great chemical adventure, which was equivalent to the revolution occurring in biology at the same time: dozens of new elements were mapped onto the Periodic Table and then experimentally combined with each other, often in ways that never happened in nature. Chlorine particularly fascinated chemists because it can combine to make thousands of long-lasting molecules, many of which are soluble in fat.

One hundred years after Scheele's discovery, chemists were still exploring chlorine's combinatory potential. Dichlorodiphenyltrichloroethane (DDT) was first synthesized in 1873 by PhD student Othmar Zeidler, who was working in the laboratory of Adolph von Bayer at the University of Strasbourg. But Zeidler failed to find any particular use for the compound, and it lay metaphorically corked in a dusty test tube for 60 years.

Müller came upon DDT during his work as a research chemist at the J. R. Geigy Company in Basel, Switzerland. He began his career with investigations of dyes and tanning agents, and his interests moved from tanning to textiles to moth protection. As a natural extension, in 1935—the year Rachel Carson began work in the U.S. Bureau of Fisheries—Müller began his search for chemicals to fight agricultural pests.

Mechanical and biological control of pests dates back at least to Roman times. According to the Roman scholar Pliny the Elder, locusts had to be picked off crops three times a year by law in Cyrene. Jays and jackdaws were valued guests on farms because they were known to eat large quantities of insects. Some Roman and Greek authors also reported the efficacy of planting vetch among cabbages to foil cabbageworm. Chemical control also dates back thousands of years: Sulfur mixed with oil was a popular insecticide in Greek and

The Romans welcomed jays on their farms because the birds gorged on insect pests. Such "biological control" was eclipsed by cheap and potent chemical pesticides only in the 1950s, which, ironically, poisoned natural predators.

A vedalia beetle at work. The beetle was imported from Australia to control scale insects, and helped save the California citrus industry in the 1880s. Carson wrote approvingly of "biological control."

Roman times. Plant extracts and bitumen were also widely used. In the Middle Ages, chemical control if anything went backward, as mainland Europe resorted to excommunicating insects in surprisingly frequent religious show trials. In the sixteenth century alone, 18 trials of insect pests took place.

By the early nineteenth century, scientists had begun to supplement naturally occurring insecticides such as tobacco, and herbicides such as lime and salt, with a range of chemical treatments. Paris green—a mixture of copper, acetic acid, and arsenic—was accidentally found to protect grapes from attack. Copper sulfate came into use to protect wheat from charlock. Hydrocyanic acid, carbon bisulfide, and lead arsenate were also used as the farmer's chemical arsenal rapidly expanded.

There were also advances in biological methods of pest control. One of the most dramatic tests took place in 1873 in California, where an infestation of cottony cushion scale was crushed by releasing huge numbers of vedalia beetles introduced from abroad. Nonetheless, arsenic-based pesticides remained the most popular, even though they were known to be toxic to farmers. It is ironic, considering the danger to humans of arsenic-based pesticides, that the first pesticide law in the United States was passed in 1901— as a measure against fraud—to ensure that manufacturers put *more* arsenic into their products, not less.

In the early twentieth century, most pesticide research focused on more efficient and safer ways to apply these toxic pesticides. But a few chemists, such as Müller, became convinced that they could find synthetic substitutes. Müller drew up a wish list for the "perfect pesticide." It should, he said, have the following properties:

1. Great insect toxicity
2. Rapid onset of toxic action
3. Little or no mammalian or plant toxicity
4. No irritant effect and no (or only a faint) odor (in any case, not an unpleasant one)
5. The range of action should be as wide as possible, and cover as many Arthropoda [insects] as possible
6. Long, persistent action—i.e., good chemical stability
7. Low price

The last requirement was important—he was a competitive industrial chemist, after all, not an academic. "After the fruitless testing of hundreds of various substances," Müller later said, "it was not easy to discover a good contact insecticide." Four years into his search, in September 1939, he decided to try out DDT. It was almost perfect as a pesticide. It met most of his criteria, although he worried that the white granules were slow to take effect. Yet it was undoubtedly potent. "My fly cage was so toxic after a short period," he recalled, "that even after very thorough cleaning of the cage, untreated flies, on touching the walls, fell to the floor. I could carry on my trials only after dismantling the cage, having it thoroughly cleaned, and after that leaving it for about one month in the open air." He had found his "perfect pesticide."

Of Lice and Men: DDT in World War II

The Swiss government immediately tested DDT against the Colorado potato beetle. It worked. Products containing DDT came onto the market in Switzerland in 1941. The U.S. Department of Agriculture was also quick to try DDT, with successful agricultural trials in 1943. However, it was in wartime use that DDT really came into its own, against a humble but potentially deadly enemy—the louse.

> *The field of pest control is immense, and many problems impatiently await a solution. A new territory has opened up for the synthetics chemist—a territory which is still unexplored and difficult.*
>
> Paul Hermann Müller,
> Nobel Prize speech, 1948

DDT was not the only synthesized chemical to find wartime applications. German scientists, in the course of developing agents of chemical warfare, discovered many other compounds that were lethal to insects. In fact, insects were often used to test chemicals as agents of death for man. For example, a phosphorus compound developed by Gerhard Schrader in the late 1930s was found to be toxic to insects. The Nazis were so interested in the potential of "E 605" that the German company Bayer continued its work in secret. Their interest was not academic: The same company chemists developed Zyklon-B gas, which was deployed in Nazi death camps to kill millions. After the war, E 605 saw a new incarnation as the pesticide Parathion.

DDT's wartime application, in contrast, was a humanitarian one. Lice, as carriers of typhus, were responsible for the deaths of more than 5 million people during World War I, and the Allied command feared a

A GI is sprayed against body lice. DDT and other pesticides were credited with saving many military and civilian lives in World War II.

repetition of such a disaster during World War II. As the Allies prepared their invasion of Italy in late 1943, a typhus epidemic seemed imminent in Naples. In January 1944, the outbreak was quashed after all civilians and occupying Allied troops were sprayed with a DDT treatment. This was the first time a winter typhus epidemic had been stopped in its tracks. DDT was then used to clear South Pacific islands of mosquitoes for U.S. troops, and also in parts of the Mediterranean affected by malaria, both during and after the war.

Müller received the Nobel Prize for Physiology or Medicine in 1948, "for his discovery of the high efficiency of DDT as a contact poison against several arthropods." The award primarily recognized the many civilian lives DDT saved during and after the war, not its use as an agricultural pest control, which had been the original motivation for the research. Müller was feted as a hero. "DDT kills the fly; it kills the mosquito, which spreads malaria; the louse, which spreads typhus; the flea, which spreads the plague; and the sandfly, which spreads tropical diseases," Gustaf Hellström of the Swedish Royal Academy of Sciences told Müller at the Nobel banquet. "In the mind of the layman you stand out as a benefactor of mankind of such stature that you may well also need the humility of a saint to escape falling victim to the worst of all spiritual diseases—*hubris*."

Müller displayed some modesty, as befitted such a highly methodical chemist—he admitted in 1948 that he still did not fully understand the exact mechanism by which DDT killed insects. But he operated within a scientific culture that did suffer from a form of *hubris,* or fatal pride. Müller gave a good example of the contemporary scientific mind-set in his Nobel speech of December 11, 1948. He approvingly quoted the German medical researcher Dr. Sigmund Frankel:

The artist sees as his purpose not the slavish imitation of nature degraded by art to simple reproduction. He rather employs his subjective conception of beauty in order to give birth to a new beauty which nature does not offer in precisely that form. He creates this by using a natural form of representation which is nonetheless characteristic of the artist. Similarly the synthetics chemist must create new types of substances … In so doing, his imagination, too, must be given full rein, just as the artist creates from contemplation of what, subjectively, appears to him as being beautiful.

Inventor Thomas Midgley was heralded as brilliant in his lifetime but later blamed for the environmental problems caused by his two greatest innovations: leaded gasoline and ozone-depleting chemicals.

Many of the synthetic chemicals created during the chemical revolution of the 1930s and 1940s later came to be seen as mixed blessings. Euphoric inventors were solving problems and creating them at the same time. The American engineer and inventor Thomas Midgley (1889–1944) spent six years of his life solving the problem of "knocking" in gasoline engines, succeeding finally by adding triethyl lead. Later, in just three days he solved the problem of poisonous leaks from refrigeration units by inventing CFCs (chlorofluorocarbons) as a new generation of refrigerants. It was only decades later that lead in gasoline was shown to

Federal agents seize 100,000 bottles of contraband liquor on 51st Street, Manhattan, in 1935. Unscrupulous bootleggers sometimes used toxic chemicals to make counterfeit liquor.

be damaging to brain development, and that CFCs were found to be the main cause of the "ozone hole" *(see pages 109–110)*. "Midgley changed American life twice," says John Lienhard of the University of Houston. "Both times his inventive heritage was life-threatening."

Other "beautiful" creations that turned out to be persistent pollutants included polychlorinated biphenyls (PCBs, used in electrical appliances and widely manufactured in the United States and Europe), hexachlorobenzene (HCB, used as a fungicide for wheat, and also in industry in organic synthesis as a raw material for synthetic rubber), and lindane (gamma hexaclorocyclohexane, a pesticide still used for head-lice treatments today). As noted previously, not all of these inventions had innocuous beginnings: Parathion had sinister origins as the nerve poison E 605, which was developed by the German company IG Farben's subsidiary Bayer during World War II. Scientific pride in synthetic products is evident in the grandiloquent company and brand names of that time: Hercules Powder, Victor, Freon, Toxaphene.

One of the strangest tales of this period comes from 1930—during the era of Prohibition. Bootleggers soon found that Jamaican ginger made a good liquor substitute. The only problem was getting ahold of it. Some resourceful but disreputable chemists found they could make a tangy synthetic substitute by adding a phosphate chemical closely related to Parathion. Tragically, 15,000 people who drank the fake bootleg Jamaican ginger developed permanently crippling "Jamaica ginger paralysis."

Rachel Carson's Youth and Training

Rachel Louise Carson was born in 1907, the third child of Maria and Robert Carson. She grew up in Springdale, Pennsylvania, which was then an idyllic rural community of wooden houses and orchards on the banks of the Allegheny River. However, its proximity to Pittsburgh—already the iron and steel capital of North America—meant that the town was increasingly caught up in the rapid industrialization of the 1910s and 1920s. Because of large power stations at each end of the town, the Carsons experienced industrial pollution firsthand.

Rachel early on was delighted by the wonders of the natural world, bird-watching and pondering over fossilized shells with her mother, Maria, a dedicated follower of the nature-study movement. As soon as she could read, Rachel was captivated by animal tales—especially the rabbits of Beatrix Potter; and Toad, Mole, and Rat of Kenneth Grahame's *The Wind in the Willows* (1908). It was not long before she was writing animal stories herself.

Carson was also an avid reader of the popular children's magazine *St. Nicholas*, and her first story was published in the magazine when she was 11 years old. In being published by *St. Nicholas* magazine, she joined the ranks of young writers as diverse as William Faulkner, F. Scott Fitzgerald, and e. e. cummings. But she outdid these three boy prodigies by having four stories published

> *Remember, I prophesy you'll be a famous author yet. Please don't take all the frogs and skeletons too seriously.*
>
> Marjorie Stevenson,
> school friend, 1929

within a year, earning her first ten dollars as well as three awards. Furthermore, these were not stories about cuddly animals—they were war stories.

In 1921 Rachel Carson was a solitary teenager devouring everything she could find to read about the ocean—from *Moby Dick* to *Treasure Island*—and as a published and paid writer, she began to turn her literary attentions to the natural world. She won a scholarship to Pennsylvania College for Women (PCW, later to become Chatham College). In an introductory essay, she wrote, "I love all the beautiful things of nature, and the wild creatures are my friends."

Mary Scott Skinker was Rachel's charismatic biology teacher at PCW. Her glamor, panache, and intellectual brilliance fascinated Carson, and biology opened up new avenues for Carson's love of nature. Carson was reading Alfred, Lord Tennyson's poem "Locksley Hall" during a thunderstorm. When she came to the line "For the mighty

Top left: "I read a great deal almost from infancy," said Rachel Carson, here aged around five with the family dog Candy. She was writing her own stories by the age of eight and was first published three years later.

Above: Carson with her mother, Maria McLean Carson, in the mid-1920s. Her mother gave her a love of nature and writing from an early age, and remained a close companion until her death in 1958.

21

Carson takes notes on the dock at Woods Hole, 1950. Her investigations at the Marine Biological Laboratory in 1929 confirmed a lifelong fascination with the sea and led to two best-selling books on the oceans.

wind arises, roaring seaward, and I go," she realized that her future lay with the sea—even though she had never seen it.

Passionate about writing, Rachel Carson soon faced a difficult decision: whether to switch from English to science as a major. In early 1928, she decided to go for science, turning her back—so she thought—on writing. She planned a master's degree in zoology to follow a bachelor's in biology. She was ambitious, knowing—as her biographer, Linda Lear, writes—that "comparatively few women succeeded in moving to the front ranks of science in the 1920s and 1930s, either in teaching or research." If anything, the situation was becoming even less promising for women: the Great Depression saw major cutbacks in scientific research, limiting opportunities for all scientists, even men. Men were also taking over as heads of faculty in women's colleges such as PCW.

Carson graduated magna cum laude from PCW and won a scholarship to do her master's degree at Johns Hopkins. Her research topic was to be the comparative anatomy of the turtle's cranium. In the summer of 1929 she spent six weeks as a "beginning investigator" at the Marine Biological Laboratory at Woods Hole, Massachusetts. The atmosphere at Woods Hole was relaxed, clubby, welcoming toward women. Carson began to meet scientists from the U.S. Bureau of Fisheries and spent a lot of time at low tide on the seashore. Her fascination with marine biology had begun.

At Johns Hopkins, Carson had the opportunity to study under the pioneering geneticist H. S. Jennings and also work as a lab assistant for the maverick human biologist Raymond Pearl. At the same time, Carson—under duress—took an organic chemistry course, one of only two women in a class of 70. It was to be her first insight into the rarified world of the chemist, and she was not greatly impressed, although she passed the course easily.

Pressed for both time and money, Rachel Carson struggled to find a subject for her thesis at Johns Hopkins—first turtles, then pit vipers, then flying squirrels—before finally completing an essay on catfish kidneys in 1932, to pass her master's degree. Despite teaching appointments, recurrent financial problems forced her to drop out of the PhD program in mid-1934. The Great Depression was not a great time for a young female scientific researcher to be seeking work, so she was fortunate to get part-time work with Elmer Higgins at the U.S. Bureau of Fisheries Educational Division, writing a series of short radio programs on marine life.

Under the Sea-Wind: the Lyrical Marine Ecologist

This was the start of a creative period for Rachel Carson, writing popular accounts of marine science both for the Bureau of Fisheries and also frequently for papers such as the *Baltimore Sunday Sun*. She deepened her knowledge of the sea, notably around Chesapeake Bay. Her popular science was published under the name R. L. Carson so that readers would assume male authorship. And when her essay

Elmer Higgins of the U.S. Bureau of Fisheries hired Carson in 1935, telling her, "I've never seen a written word of yours, but I'm going to take a sporting chance." It paid off handsomely—Carson stayed in the service until 1952.

It is Miss Carson's particular gift to be able to blend scientific knowledge with the spirit of poetic awareness, thus restoring to us a true sense of the world.

Henry Beston, 1952

Manuscript page of *Under the Sea-Wind* (1941). Carson's book brought marine animals to life for the general public, without resorting to cute but unscientific techniques. The book was eclipsed during World War II but later sold well.

"Undersea" was accepted by the *Atlantic Monthly* in 1937, she knew that the choice to be scientist or writer had turned out to be a false one—she had become both.

She and the publisher Simon & Schuster were soon courting each other for a book on the sea. She wanted to capture the poetic and accessible style of authors such as Henry Williamson *(see page 10)* but was too much the scientist to resort to giving animals human characteristics. Carson's *Under the Sea-Wind* (1941) succeeded in its lyrical and convincingly ecological celebration of seabirds, mackerel, and eel. But events at Pearl Harbor drowned out her good reviews.

During and after the war, Carson continued to produce a wide range of publications for the now merged Fish and Wildlife Service (FWS), including a series called *Conservation in Action* that enabled her to travel widely around U.S. wildlife refuges and explore her developing ecological understanding. On one trip she visited the Sheepscot River on the Maine coast. This magical place was to become a source of inspiration for the rest of her life.

Her access to FWS research also enabled her to place topical articles elsewhere. In 1945 she offered a piece on recent tests on DDT to the *Reader's Digest*, which was declined. Her personal writing also included a prizewinning "conservation pledge" for *Outdoor Life* magazine—a sign of her growing ecological consciousness. Toward the end of the 1940s, Carson was also steadily collecting material for a second book on the sea, capitalizing on the major scientific advances emerging from classified research during the war.

In 1948 Carson signed up with an ambitious literary agent, Marie Rodell, who immediately helped her win a Saxton Fellowship to give her writing time. Rodell placed the manuscript of *The Sea Around Us* with Oxford University Press (OUP). Rumor had it that the book was rejected by 20 other publishers—in fact, OUP was the second in line. *The New Yorker* serialized most of the book, starting in June 1951, and the book was published a month later.

Amid the anxieties of the Korean War and McCarthy's Communist witch hunts, readers found solace in Carson's ecological perspective. *The Sea Around Us* was an instant best seller, winning her a cluster of awards, rave reviews, and financial independence. It also evoked sexist comments, questioning how such a work could have been written by a woman, especially at a time when her family life was compromised by her unmarried niece's pregnancy. She was, however, financially secure enough to resign her post at the FWS in mid-1952, which gave her time to get started on a new book.

The town of Wiscasset, Maine, on the banks of the Sheepscot River. Carson fell in love with the Maine coast around the Sheepscot, a far cry from her increasingly polluted birthplace in Allegheny County, Pennsylvania.

Accepting the National Book Award in 1952, Carson spoke out against the assumption "that knowledge of science is the prerogative of only a small number of human beings, isolated and priestlike in their laboratories. That is not true. It cannot be true." She might well have been thinking of the chemists who were then preparing to go to war on America's pests.

America's War on Pests

Once World War II ended, large stockpiles of DDT were made available in hot climates for public health purposes, particularly against malaria-carrying mosquitoes. DDT spraying, combined with drainage, succeeded in banishing malaria from the southern United States. Elsewhere in the world, the results were even more dramatic. In 1943 Venezuela had more than 8 million cases of malaria; by 1958 the number of cases was only 800. India, which had more than 10 million cases of malaria in 1935, had 286,000 in 1969. In Italy, where DDT had its first public health application, malaria fell most dramatically, from 412,000 cases at the end of the war to just 37 in 1968. In 1969, the World Health Organization (WHO) issued a statement to the effect that it was

> *proud of its amazing record of having been the
> main agent in eradicating malaria in countries
> whose populations total 550 million people, of
> having saved about 5 million lives and prevented
> 100 million illnesses in the first eight years of its
> use ... without causing the loss of a single life
> by poisoning from DDT alone.*

Today, the World Health Organization credits DDT with saving between 50 and 100 million lives from malaria, but the current Roll Back Malaria program supported by WHO in fact has an ambivalent attitude toward whether the pesticide should still be used in developing countries. Some experts say it must be phased out, others that it still has a role to play *(see pages 115–116)*.

Airplanes were used for spraying DDT against mosquitoes in Europe in 1945. Aerial spraying of pesticides for disease control and crop protection soon became widespread in the United States.

DDT was soon not just, or even primarily, used to save human lives. It was also used in developed countries—especially the United States—to control insect pests that attacked agricultural crops. Despite all efforts by farmers, pests annually destroy about one-third of all crops worldwide. After the food is harvested, insects, micro-organisms, rodents, and birds inflict a further 10–20 percent loss, bringing total losses to between 40 and 50 percent. By 1952, insects, weeds, and disease cost U.S. farmers an estimated $13 billion in crops annually, out of a gross annual agricultural output of $31 billion.

It is not surprising that U.S. farmers quickly adopted DDT and its synthetic relatives, replacing the old-fashioned and dangerous arsenic-based pesticides. Early testing by the U.S. Public Health Service and the Food and Drug Administration's Division of Pharmacology had found no serious human toxicity problems with DDT, and there had been no reports of problems from wartime use. Initially it was used on fruit trees and on vegetable crops, and subsequently on cotton. Thanks to the huge surplus of planes after the war, aerial spraying became increasingly affordable and popular—and DDT was well suited to aerial spraying because of its persistence even when applied thinly to foliage.

One in seven families in the United States lived and worked on farms in 1950. The Great Depression, which had been especially tough on farmers, was a vivid memory, immortalized by John Steinbeck's *The Grapes of Wrath* and Walker Evans's photographs of sharecroppers. Although U.S. citizens had not

Photographs of rural poverty, like this one of a poor sharecropping family in the Great Depression of the 1930s, shocked the public, and led to support for industrial agriculture with massive use of pesticides.

experienced the level of food shortages seen in Europe during the war, there was a general determination that the United States should be a land of plenty—especially in food, but in lumber and cotton too. Pests were not going to get in the way of progress. It is difficult to exaggerate the sheer enthusiasm for technological solutions at the time. A *Scientific American* article by Francis Joseph Weiss was typical of the early 1950s. "Chemical agriculture, still in its infancy, should eventually advance our agricultural efficiency at least as much as machines have in the past 150 years," claimed Weiss. "Farming is being revolutionized by new fertilizers, insecticides, fungicides, weedkillers, leaf removers, soil conditioners, plant hormones, trace minerals, antibiotics, and synthetic milk for pigs."

The production of synthetic pesticides like DDT in the United States soared from 124 million pounds (56,245,454 kg) in 1947 to 638 million pounds (289,391,932 kg) by 1960—a fivefold rise. This was influenced by such factors as a general rise in chemical use in farming, as well as the upsurge of accidentally introduced pests such as fire ants *(see page 29)*, gypsy moths *(see page 32)*, and Dutch elm disease *(see page 47)*. When *Silent Spring* was published in 1962, some 500 compounds, in more than 54,000 formulations, were registered for use as pesticides in the country; Rachel Carson estimated that the wholesale value of these was well over $250 million—equivalent to $1.4 billion in today's prices. Carson also noted that "in the plans and hopes of the industry this enormous production is only a beginning." An unprecedented increase in agricultural productivity was taking place, spurred by improvements in farming practices and technologies, and by reduced pest-related losses because of use of the synthetic pesticides.

In the postwar years, farmers, and the U.S. Department of Agriculture (USDA), quickly saw the potential of DDT to deal with a wide range of insect pests. Take the case of the fire ant, imported inadvertently from Brazil sometime after World War I. Its foot-high nests irritated tractor drivers, but it was not perceived as a serious pest. Yet in 1957, the USDA drew up plans for an eradication program that would involve spraying 20 million acres across nine Southern states—not just audacious in its scope but also highly lucrative for the pesticide industry.

Not So Perfect Pesticides

Doubts within the scientific community were raised about DDT even before Müller won his Nobel Prize in 1948. In 1945, the Fish and Wildlife Service (FWS) and other organizations were beginning to ask questions about DDT. Researcher John George documented the immediate deaths of fish and birds after spraying at Clear Lake Junction, New York, as early as 1946. Some pest insect populations had also started to develop resistance to DDT, decreasing its effectiveness and leading farmers to apply greater and greater amounts of insecticide, particularly on cotton fields.

On December 15, 1945, R. A. M. Case wrote a paper on the "Toxic Effects of DDT in Man" for the *British Medical Journal.* He described an experiment that sounds bizarre to

Trials of DDT to kill the corn borer pest are conducted in El Paso, Illinois, in 1946. The pest caused millions of dollars of damage a year, but Carson was critical of the effectiveness of chemical control programs like this.

modern ears. Two Royal Navy researchers pressed their bare skin up against walls painted with DDT dissolved in water-based paint and covered with a thick layer of oil. They reported: "The tiredness, heaviness, and aching of limbs were very real things, and the mental state was also most distressing." The pair also experienced "extreme irritability … great distaste for work of any sort … a feeling of mental incompetence in tackling the simplest mental task. The joint pains were quite violent at times."

Human testing of pesticides was commonplace up until the 1970s, with researchers often finding their human guinea pigs among the prison population. *Silent Spring* recounts many tragic stories about human testing—such as the researcher who exposed himself to a tiny amount of one pesticide and was overcome by its toxic effects before he could reach for the antidote he had so carefully prepared. Rachel Carson was particularly damning of Dr. Wayland Hayes, chief toxicologist of the U.S. Public Health Service. Hayes conducted experiments in which 51 volunteers began eating meals laced with DDT. Few completed the course, and Carson was outraged at the lack of follow-up monitoring.

The Reluctant Campaigner: From Tide Pools to Manifesto

Carson enjoyed the opportunity *The Sea Around Us* gave her to speak out against humankind's destructiveness. This book eventually sold more than a million copies and became the *only* "green" book to make it onto the top ten annual

best-seller lists compiled by *Publishers Weekly* from 1950 to today (even *Silent Spring* did not manage this). She won a Guggenheim fellowship to write her third book, an ecological guide to the seashore called *The Edge of the Sea*, which was published to critical acclaim in 1955.

Meanwhile, she was becoming engaged in the rapidly growing conservation movement. Her commitment had been building steadily for a decade, but was accelerated through enlightened self-interest—to protect the woods around her new vacation home in West Southport, Maine. She joined the Wilderness Society (founded in 1935), maintained her involvement in the Audubon Society, and networked with private philanthropists. She also became involved in the Nature Conservancy, a not-for-profit group established in 1951. "Our lives are enriched by understanding the close interrelationship between living things and their environment," she told a handful of farsighted and energetic locals thinking of setting up a Maine chapter in September 1956. "The Nature Conservancy appeals because it is the only group known which is actually preserving areas." She was named honorary chairwoman soon after its founding and bore the title proudly until her death.

When John F. Kennedy was elected president in 1960, conservation gained still more in popularity. Kennedy and Interior Secretary Stewart L. Udall began to voice concern over pollution and the loss of wilderness, and they proposed establishing a fund to finance further expansion of federally protected lands. "Many nations no longer have the

Rachel Carson spent whole days and sometimes nights exploring tidepools for marine specimens, as seen here in 1955 with wildlife artist Bob Hines. Her firsthand ecological awareness was key to the success of her books.

Above left: **The gypsy moth is an enemy of U.S. trees. Efforts in the 1950s to eradicate it by aerial spraying of insecticides alarmed naturalists and inspired Rachel Carson to write** Silent Spring.

Above right: **Spraying for gypsy moths is done over Ocean Township, New Jersey, in 1991. Carson would have been horrified at continuing spraying, though modern pesticides are less damaging.**

option of preserving part of their land in pristine condition," wrote Udall in *The Quiet Crisis* (1963), an environmental advocacy book written while he was still Interior Secretary. "We must take ours up before it is too late. A wilderness system will offer man what many consider the supreme human experience."

Udall focused mainly on human threats to wilderness. But the pristine forests were also under attack by one of the worst U.S. imports—the gypsy moth. Leopold Trouvelot, a professional artist and amateur entomologist, had brought over gypsy moths from France, planning to crossbreed them with silkworms in an attempt to establish a U.S. silk industry. They had managed to escape in 1869 from his lab in Medford, Massachusetts.

The gypsy moth spread slowly through New England, but a basket of control measures, including natural predators, quarantine, and local spraying, had more or less contained its advance beyond the Adirondacks by 1955. The decision the following year to start a massive aerial spraying campaign to try to eradicate—rather than contain—the gypsy moth therefore represented a major change in policy by the USDA's Plant Pest Control Division. In 1956 nearly a million acres (4,045 sq km) of forest across Michigan, Pennsylvania, New Jersey, and New York were sprayed with DDT dissolved in fuel oil. In 1957 plans were announced to spray a further 3 million acres (12,140 sq km). To block the additional spraying over their homes, a group of eminent Long Islanders, including ornithologist Robert Cushman Murphy, formed the Committee Against Mass Poisoning. A court case followed, publicizing evidence of contamination and displaying the high-handed reaction of government to citizen protest. The court case ran on into 1960, finally making it to the Supreme Court, where it was eventually thrown out on a technicality. After the Long Islanders failed to obtain a court injunction preventing it, suburban fields, backyards, and meadows were sprayed, in addition to the moths' usual forest habitat.

Irston Barnes, of the Washington, D.C., Audubon Society, who was also critical of the fire ant eradication program *(see page 29)*, first alerted Carson to the USDA's vainglorious pest-control plans. What really incensed her, however, was a copy of an angry letter about the East Coast "mass poisoning" that had been published in the *Boston Herald* on January 12, 1958. It was sent to her by a friend, Olga Owens Huckins, who enclosed the story of her own experience of songbird deaths following spraying in New England against moths and mosquitoes. By February 1, 1958, Carson had made some inquiries, grown suspicious, felt she had "struck what appears to be 'pay dirt,'" and was determined to write about the spraying.

Cranberries growing in a bog. The Great Cranberry Scandal of 1959 raised awareness of pesticide pollution, though presidential rivals John F. Kennedy and Richard Nixon tried to downplay alarm.

By all accounts, the spraying contractors—paid by the gallon, not the acre—often behaved recklessly, and public officials responded arrogantly to any challenge. Beekeepers suffered immediately after the spraying, since bees are as susceptible to DDT as other insects are. But market gardeners and dairy farmers were also hard hit by economic losses from DDT residues: Produce such as lettuces were "burned" by the pesticide, peas were testing three times the legal maximum, and no residues at all were permitted in milk for interstate trade. One well-connected woman—Marjorie Spock, the sister of Dr. Benjamin Spock—had a 2-acre (0.01 sq km) garden that was sprayed 14 times in a single day (until then, it had been one of the very few organic gardens in the United States). Many other people were distressed by the immediate loss of wildlife in their gardens and worried about the effects on human health.

No industrial accident, scientific paper, or lawsuit would do as much to prepare ordinary Americans for *Silent Spring* as did the Great Cranberry Scandal of 1959. The new herbicide aminotriazole, or amitrol, was registered with the USDA in 1956 for nonfood use and later for use on cranberry bogs—on condition that it was applied after harvest. Yet, in 1957 some growers in the Pacific Northwest applied the pesticide before harvesting. When the chemical compound was subsequently found in cranberries, the FDA recalled much of the Northwest crop from market, because no safe level of residue had been established.

As Thanksgiving 1959 approached, toxicity tests confirmed early fears: the herbicide was found to be carcinogenic in tests on laboratory rats. Despite efforts by the National Cranberry Association to recall all suspect shipments, contaminated batches got through. Health Education and Welfare Secretary Arthur S. Flemming announced a ban on all cranberries until the industry could guarantee effective removal of contaminated berries. New England growers, whose berries were untainted, were outraged—and there was political infighting, too. Voters were treated to the spectacle of presidential candidates Richard Nixon and John F. Kennedy courageously cramming their mouths full of cranberries to win over rural voters—one of the earliest-known instances of this type of electoral gimmick.

An American family enjoys a Thanksgiving dinner. The public was horrified to discover in 1959 that cranberry sauce might be contaminated by the pesticide amitrol.

The public was not fooled. The scandal revealed major loopholes in the government's regulation of pesticides. In November 1959, Carson and colleagues attended the hearings on the FDA's cranberry ban. She was struck by the poor quality of the evidence presented by the pesticide industry—and awed by their arrogance and financial muscle. These were lessons she took carefully on board as she started in earnest on the research that would lead to *Silent Spring*.

UNDERSTANDING
RACHEL CARSON'S *SILENT SPRING*
THE BOOK

The success of *Silent Spring* owes much to Rachel Carson's talent for research and for synthesizing and presenting complex information in a clear and accessible fashion. But it also owes more than a little to timing.

The opportunity—Carson saw it as a duty, too—to write about pesticide problems could not have come at a better time for her. Carson once commented that books find their authors, and this was the case with *Silent Spring*. In the late 1950s, she had written three poetic, popular treatments of the science of the sea. She was beginning to feel she might have exhausted the possibilities of the genre, but hadn't found a new one, and was in danger of frittering away her talents on well-paid but uninspired compilations and similar writing projects.

> *We don't usually think of* The New Yorker *as changing the world, but this is one time it might.*
>
> William Shawn, editor of *The New Yorker*, 1958

In early 1957, *Silent Spring* was no more than an outline for an article on the problems of aerial spraying and the Long Island court case about aerial spraying in residential areas *(see page 33)*. Carson submitted her idea to E.B. White, a staff writer for *The New Yorker* and a distinguished naturalist, suggesting that he take it on. Fortunately for her, he declined, advising her to accept the challenge herself. Carson also worked up a book idea and then presented it to Houghton Mifflin. She initially planned to collaborate with an ambitious but far from like-minded young reporter named Edwin Diamond, a departure from her successful writing mode. Diamond, a science editor at *Newsweek*, was keen to collaborate with the

E.B. White and his canine critic at work for *The New Yorker*, 1955. White later told Carson her book "will be an *Uncle Tom's Cabin* of a book—the sort that will help turn the tide."

award-winning writer; Carson believed that Diamond would be able to undertake much of the legwork and also gain access to detailed material relating to the Long Island lawsuit. William Shawn, editor of *The New Yorker*, came back first to Carson, intrigued, and asked for a two-part piece of 20,000 to 30,000 words. Growing ever more interested, he soon returned with a request for 50,000 words in three installments—approaching the length of a full-size book.

Meanwhile, Diamond had proved to be unsuitable as a collaborator—his input was not what Carson was looking for, and Diamond did not share Carson's critical stance against the pesticide industry. As a result, Diamond was cut out of the book deal with Houghton Mifflin, leading to lasting animosity on his part. (Later Diamond, then senior editor at *Newsweek*, was to write a dismissive essay on *Silent Spring* in the *Saturday Evening Post*, accusing Carson of being McCarthyite in her vilification of scientists.)

Carson began to piece together her material in characteristically meticulous fashion. She built up an ever-widening network of supportive researchers, including Bob Rudd, an enthusiastic young ecologist specializing in the impact of pesticides on wildlife, and Malcolm Hargraves, a leukemia specialist at the Mayo Clinic. Because many scientists admired Carson's *The Sea Around Us,* they were prepared informally to provide its author with confidential information, sometimes risking their jobs in doing so. She and research assistant Bette Haney also plowed through mounds of published research. Gradually Carson tracked down the robust evidence she required—but not all was smooth sailing. Carson admitted to a friend that "the title has been a dreadful problem," her favorite clunkers ranging from *How to Balance Nature* to *The Control of Nature* to *Man Against Nature* to *Man Against the Earth* to *Dissent in Favor of Man*. It was not Carson but editor Paul Brooks and agent Marie Rodell who suggested *Silent Spring*—a title that picks up the book's most powerful warning, resonating for millions of bird lovers: a spring devoid of birdsong.

Late Spring: Delayed by Ill Health

It's an ill poison that doesn't give some publisher a good book.

Lovell Thompson,
Houghton Mifflin, 1959

Poor health meant that the book was severely delayed, even by Carson's normal standards. In early 1960, Carson was beset by a duodenal ulcer, followed by pneumonia, and then in March, she underwent a radical mastectomy after discovering a tumor in her breast. It was not until December 1960 that she discovered the tumor was malignant—the doctor had concealed this from her at the time of the operation. Her writing progress was literally painstaking, causing friends alarm and anxiety, and logistical difficulties for her agent, Marie Rodell, and editor, Paul Brooks. As Carson wrote to close friend Dorothy Freeman:

> *Yes, there is quite a story behind* Silent Spring, *isn't there? Such a catalog of illnesses! If one were superstitious it would be easy to believe in some malevolent influence at work, determined by some means to keep the book from being finished.*

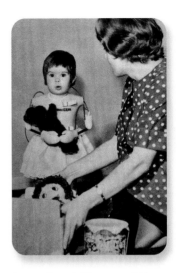

The mother of this young girl born without arms in Stockholm, 1963, had taken the drug thalidomide during pregnancy. The scandal horrified the North American and European public.

Yet every month that she fell further behind made what she was writing more timely. There is a real possibility that if *Silent Spring* had been completed on schedule in February 1960, it would have fallen on deaf, or at least less receptive, ears. But by mid-1962, when the book eventually came out, the evidence about the dangers of pesticides was more compelling, and the American public was more sensitive to the issue of airborne danger and invisible toxins. It was only in 1957 that the Soviet Union first demonstrated ICBM (Intercontinental Ballistic Missile) capability, leading to widespread fear of nuclear war. By the turn of the decade, researchers had found strontium-90 in babies' teeth, and fear of fallout was universal. Bomb shelters were built across the country. Tensions heightened in 1960 when a U2 spy plane was shot down, and the Soviet Union shipped missiles to Fidel Castro's Cuba. By the summer of 1962, another spate of nuclear tests were taking place at the Nevada test site. At this stage there were few direct protests about nuclear testing, but the ubiquitous image of the mushroom cloud entered the popular consciousness at the same time as fears about aerial spraying were growing.

The thalidomide scandal also prepared the ground for *Silent Spring*. This drug was widely prescribed to pregnant women in Western Europe and Canada in the late 1950s, and was even distributed as samples in the United States, though never approved by the FDA. Tragically, it was soon shown to cause serious birth defects and was

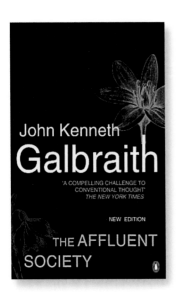

John Kenneth Galbraith's best-selling attack on American consumerism was published in 1958. Critics called him a snob, but Galbraith went on to advise J.F.K. on economics, and became ambassador to India.

withdrawn from the market in late 1961. Although Carson does not mention thalidomide in the book, she and her readership were conscious of the parallels—an arrogant and impetuous medical establishment, excessive claims for a new "wonder chemical," lack of careful testing, and thousands of children the innocent victims.

While she was working on *Silent Spring*, Carson had an opportunity to observe critical reaction to two groundbreaking environmental books: William Longgood's *The Poisons in Your Food* (1960) and Murray Bookchin's *Our Synthetic Environment* (1962), published under the pseudonym Lewis Herber. Carson was also reading more widely around her subject—for example, Harvard professor John Kenneth Galbraith's critique of mass consumerism, *The Affluent Society* (1958). Such books were to shape her views about consumerism and the relations between science and industry.

It was not just the book's scientific content that benefited from the additional time. Carson's writing style had always demanded long gestation. She wrote and rewrote, often reading whole passages out loud for rhythm and alliteration—a task her indomitable mother used to undertake for her well into her eighties. Researcher Bette Haney wondered if Carson would ever finish.

Carson was also worried about the possibility of libel actions brought by the chemical companies, so she went through the manuscript with a fine-toothed comb to remove any potentially actionable mentions of companies or brand names. She marshaled her evidence carefully, compiling a detailed list of principal sources, before getting legal opinion from Houghton Mifflin's in-house legal team. She also gathered a group of experts who read and approved part or all of the manuscript, and sent dozens of proof copies to opinion formers. Eventually, she felt confident that everything was in place.

The New Yorker articles finally hit the newsstands in June 1962, and the book was launched in September. By Christmas it had already sold more than 106,000 copies. At Carson's death in 1964, it had sold more than a million copies, and within the first decade of its publication it was translated into 16 languages. Apparently, the Kremlin immediately had *Silent Spring* secretly translated: 200 numbered copies were distributed as required reading for the Politburo and senior apparatchiks. The book has been continuously in print ever since, and has now sold more than 2 million copies. Impressive as they are, these numbers alone do not explain the book's enduring impact.

The Book in Outline

After opening with a "A Fable for Tomorrow," about the desecration of the natural world *(see pages 44–46)*, Rachel Carson makes clear, over 16 chapters, that "the central problem of our age has … become the contamination of man's total environment with such substances of incredible potential for harm." The second chapter of the book draws an analogy between pesticides and nuclear fallout and sets out Carson's position: not that "chemical insecticides must never be used," but that "a citizen shall be secure against lethal poisons," especially in his or her own home. The third chapter, "Elixirs of Death," remains one of the few comprehensible explanations of how pesticides work in English literature.

The following seven chapters deal with the numerous environmental problems in water, on land, and "Indiscriminately from the Skies." Here readers learn how pesticides cause the deaths of countless salmon, songbirds, shellfish, and even a horse.

In Chapter 11, "Beyond the Dreams of the Borgias," readers move from the natural world to the kitchen. Here, Carson presents two particularly electrifying facts: Every restaurant meal contains DDT; and Inuits who were hospitalized in Anchorage became contaminated with DDT simply by eating processed hospital food rather than their normal diet of foods, which came from as-yet uncontaminated land. The following three chapters evaluate the human cost of pesticides and in particular explore the controversial links to cancer.

The penultimate chapter describes how insects and other pests have reacted to the chemical onslaught, with many populations developing resistance to pesticides. The final chapter highlights "The Other Road"—alternatives to chemical pesticides being developed by innovative scientists—and it finishes with a resounding attack on the "Neanderthal" pesticide industry behind the Silent Spring.

On Carson's Writing Style

There are numerous essays, books, and even PhD dissertations on Carson's use of rhetoric and metaphor in *Silent Spring*, some longer than the book itself. It has kept such literary critics as Paul Brooks, Craig Waddell, and dozens of others busy. The recurrent references to nuclear fallout and the Cold War have been minutely examined. So, too, have her clever alliterations: "lethal lawns" and "shadow of sterility" are two especially memorable ones. After more than 40 years, the effect hasn't worn off, judging by Maurice Riordan's 2004 anthology of writings inspired by *Silent Spring*.

One stylistic feature of the book deserves mention here. Again and again, Carson juxtaposes ordinary housewives with men of science and business. The housewives speak at length, individually, in simple words, and are identified by hometown or name. By contrast, the "control men," "the cattlemen," "the sportsmen," "the chemical salesmen," "the town fathers," and "the federal field men" are gray, faceless, unquoted, and nameless. The repeated use of this device, counterpointing the personal with the impersonal, housewives with male technocrats, is one of the most mesmerizing features of the book, drawing in individual readers. But it was also a risky stylistic device, for many critics accused her of being one-sided and manipulative because of it.

Carson's writing in *Silent Spring* is both powerful and accurate, as evidenced even in the following key passages. But there really is no substitute for reading *Silent Spring* itself, as millions of readers have found.

A domestic scene in the 1950s. *Silent Spring* gave voice for the first time to the fears of ordinary American women about both wildlife destruction and human cancer. Carson herself ran an unconventional household.

A Fable for Tomorrow

There was once a town in the heart of America where all life seemed to live in harmony with its surroundings. The town lay in the midst of a checkerboard of prosperous farms, with fields of grain and hillsides of orchards where, in spring, white clouds of bloom drifted above the green fields. In autumn, oak and maple and birch set up a blaze of color that flamed and flickered across a backdrop of pines. Then foxes barked in the hills and deer silently crossed the fields, half hidden in the mists of the autumn mornings.

Along the roads, laurel, viburnum and alder, great ferns and wildflowers delighted the traveler's eye through much of the year. Even in winter the roadsides were places of beauty, where countless birds came to feed on the berries and on the seedheads of the dried weeds rising above the snow. The countryside was, in fact, famous for the abundance and variety of its bird life, and when the flood of migrants was pouring through in spring and autumn people traveled from great distances to observe them. Others came to fish the streams, which flowed clear and cold out of the hills and contained shady pools where trout lay. So it had been from the days many years ago when the first settlers raised their houses, sunk their wells, and built their barns.

Then a strange blight crept over the area and everything began to change. Some evil spell had settled on the community: mysterious maladies swept the flocks of chickens; the cattle and sheep sickened and died.

Everywhere was a shadow of death. The farmers spoke of much illness among their families. In the town the doctors had become more and more puzzled by new kinds of sickness appearing among their patients. There had been several sudden and unexplained deaths, not only among adults but even among children, who would be stricken suddenly while at play and die within a few hours.

There was a strange stillness. The birds, for example—where had they gone? Many people spoke of them, puzzled and disturbed. The feeding stations in the backyards were deserted. The few birds seen anywhere were moribund; they trembled violently and could not fly. It was a spring without voices. On the mornings that had once throbbed with the dawn chorus of robins, catbirds, doves, jays, wrens, and scores of other bird voices there was now no sound; only silence lay over the fields and woods and marsh.

On the farms the hens brooded, but no chicks hatched. The farmers complained that they were unable to raise any pigs—the litters were small and the young survived only a few days. The apple trees were coming into bloom but no bees droned among the blossoms, so there was no pollination and there would be no fruit.

The roadsides, once so attractive, were now lined with browned and withered vegetation as though swept by fire. These, too, were silent, deserted by all living things. Even the streams were now lifeless. Anglers no longer visited them, for all the fish had died.

In the gutters under the eaves and between the shingles of the roofs, a white granular powder still showed a few patches; some weeks before it had fallen like snow upon the roofs and the lawns, the fields and streams.

No witchcraft, no enemy action had silenced the rebirth of new life in this stricken world. The people had done it themselves.

This town does not actually exist, but it might easily have a thousand counterparts in America or elsewhere in the world. I know of no community that has experienced all the misfortunes I describe. Yet every one of these disasters has actually happened somewhere, and many real communities have already suffered a substantial number of them. A grim specter has crept upon us almost unnoticed, and this imagined tragedy may easily become a stark reality we all shall know.

What has already silenced the voices of spring in countless towns in America? This book is an attempt to explain.

Rachel Carson, *Silent Spring*, chapter 1

Manuscript page of the penultimate paragraphs of *Silent Spring*, where Carson calls pesticides "as crude a weapon as a caveman's club." Carson's confident writing and memorable turns of phrase helped spread the message to ordinary Americans and infuriated the chemical industry.

And No Birds Sing

Probably the most enduring chapter in *Silent Spring* is the eighth one, "And No Birds Sing." Carson's image of a country devoid of birdsong soon entered the popular consciousness as a nightmare rivaling that of nuclear winter. Her decision to focus on DDT's impact on birds was wise and heartfelt. A lifelong bird-watcher, she also knew from her board membership of the Washington, D.C., chapter of Audubon that she was in good company across the United States. Roger Tory Peterson's guides had led to an explosion of interest in birding *(see page 10)*, and in 1960 the National Audubon Society under Carl Buchheister boasted more than 30,000 members nationwide—a substantial potential audience for a book lamenting the demise of birds.

The American robin is a herald of spring but highly susceptible to poisoning by pesticides. Ironically, a freak mass roosting of robins in Nashville, Tennessee, in 1962 helped critics dispute *Silent Spring*.

"And No Birds Sing" is largely taken up with a discussion of the effects of spraying elm trees in an effort to control Dutch elm disease. Arriving inadvertently from Europe in 1930, Dutch elm disease devastated millions of the country's much-loved elms. By the early 1950s the disease had spread widely throughout the United States, and it was not long before DDT was pressed into service. But blanket spraying of affected elms by DDT was leading, Carson reported, to a dramatic decline in songbirds—especially the cherished robin. "To millions of Americans," observed Carson, "the season's first robin means that the grip of winter is broken. Its coming is an event reported in newspapers and told eagerly at the breakfast table." But at more and more American breakfast tables, the talk was turning from the end of winter to the reasons for dozens of dead robins on their front lawns. "Over increasingly large areas of the United States spring now comes unheralded by the return of birds," she wrote, "and the early mornings are strangely silent where once they were filled with the beauty of bird song."

Songbirds, Carson explained, were not being killed directly by the pesticides, but through an indirect route. Earthworms were eating fallen leaves contaminated with DDT, which accumulated in the earthworms that were then eaten by any of 40 or more species of birds, including the robin, in spring. In 1958, on the main campus of Michigan State University, not a single young robin was to be found.

Silent Spring reviews evidence of collapsing bird populations from across the United States, provided by numerous eminent (and invariably male) scientists. The science that Carson presents is complex, particularly for a general readership, but she presents it in such a way as to make it not only clear and comprehensible but also obviously relevant. "It is not an impossible step," she wrote, "from the embryology laboratory to the apple tree where a robin's nest holds its complement of blue-green eggs." As she continues with mesmerizing alliteration, "The eggs lie cold, the fires of life that flickered for a few days now extinguished."

But to the general reader the argument is driven home most convincingly by the eyewitness reports of ordinary "housewives" (as Carson herself calls them) from Illinois to Wisconsin. Carson was the first environmental scientist and writer to access the authentic voice of this large and uncharted environmentally committed group, who often found a forum in the letters pages of local newspapers. Consider the voice of this Milwaukee woman: "I am dreading the days to come soon now when many beautiful birds will be dying in our backyard. This is a pitiful, heartbreaking experience."

Eagles in Freefall

The disappearance of birdsong may have deeply moved Carson's female audience, but what really hit a raw nerve in the American male psyche was her alarming report about the decline of the bald eagle, presented in the same chapter. In one of the most compelling passages of *Silent Spring*, Carson wrote of

A bald eagle goes fishing. Not many U.S. citizens had seen bald eagles, but all were upset that this potent national emblem was in danger of extinction.

> another American bird [which] seems to be on the verge of extinction. This is the national symbol, the eagle. Its populations have dwindled alarmingly within the past decade. The facts suggest that something is at work in the eagle's environment which has virtually destroyed its ability to reproduce.

The eagle was, after all, the national emblem of the United States, and had been so for 190 years when *Silent Spring* appeared. It was chosen by the founding fathers because it is a species unique to North America. It features on one of the first banknotes issued by the Continental Congress in 1775—whereas the Stars and Stripes did not appear until 1777. By the 1950s, the eagle epitomized the frontier spirit, freedom, and masculine power and was used as an icon in American art, folklore, and music, as well as on money.

Bald eagles were once common throughout the United States. There may have been as many as half a million eagles at the time of Lewis and Clark's adventures at the start of the nineteenth century. But by the 1950s there were just 10,000 nesting pairs in the continental United States. By the time *Silent Spring* was written, they were an endangered species, with fewer than 500 pairs spotted in the early 1960s.

Humans were at the root of this disastrous decline in population, caused initially through mass shootings and destruction of habitat. By the early 1960s, use of pesticides on crops, and contamination of waterways and food sources by a wide range of poisons and pollutants, were implicated in their diminished numbers. *Silent Spring* reports on early scientific efforts to understand how pesticides damage the reproduction of eagles. A typical result: "the top of a tall Florida pine where a vast pile of twigs and sticks in ordered disorder holds three large white eggs, cold and lifeless."

Luckily, the reproductive difficulties of the bald eagle were noticed just in time. Mature eagles weigh up to 15 pounds and have a wingspan of 6–8 feet. They are monogamous and mate for life; a bald eagle will select another mate only if its faithful companion should die. The distinctive white head and tail feathers appear when the birds are 4–5 years old, and their beaks and eyes turn yellow at the same age. Because eagles have a life span of up to 40 years, and because juveniles can be readily told apart from adults even at a distance, a skilled amateur ornithologist such as Carson can easily differentiate a juvenile from a

By 1962, most U.S. bald eagles were failing to produce healthy chicks like these. Pesticides were implicated, but mechanisms like eggshell thinning were not yet understood.

mature bald eagle—and notice the absence of young. She had visited the Hawk Mountain Sanctuary in eastern Pennsylvania in the fall of 1945 on a two-day Audubon Society outing to observe hawks and eagles. Whether or not she had observed a lack of juvenile eagles on this trip, it was evident by the early 1960s that the bald eagle was in trouble. It was the fate of the eagle, as much as of any songbird, that so horrified Carson's readers.

One in Every Four

The prospect of a "silent spring"—whether through scarcity of robins or of eagles—brought Carson's message vividly home to many a suburban housewife and white-collar worker. But what she had to say about cancer really terrified ordinary Americans. The popular perception is that *Silent Spring* is a book about the impact of insecticides on plant and animal life, but in fact, Carson devoted nearly 50 pages over three chapters—"The Human Price," "Through a Narrow Window," and "One in Every Four"—to what she called "an ecology of the world within our bodies."

In these chapters, Carson reviews the major technical advances in cell biology and genetics made in the 1940s and 1950s, writing almost as though the human liver, which processes toxins in the body, is a small, complex, vital but vulnerable animal in its own right. Her habitual mistrust of scientists is clear as she points out that many "medical men" who had received their basic training earlier remained generally ignorant of these advances.

Unsuspecting beachgoers on Long Island are sprayed by DDT in 1945. By 1962, millions of Americans had been exposed to pesticide sprays. *Silent Spring* made controversial links between pesticides and cancer.

But she was not universally critical of the medical profession. For example, she refers approvingly to Professor H. J. Muller in Texas, who won the Nobel Prize for his discovery in 1927 that by exposing organisms to X rays he could produce mutations in their offspring. "In a world that soon gained unhappy familiarity with the grey rains of fallout, even the non-scientist now knows the potential results of radiation."

That chemicals operate in a way analogous to radiation is repeated again and again in the book:

It must not be overlooked that many chemicals are the partners of radiation, producing precisely the same effects.

Again the parallel between chemicals and radiation is exact and inescapable.

The fact that chemicals play a role similar to radiation has scarcely dawned on the public mind, nor on the minds of most medical or scientific workers.

Carson cites the American Cancer Society estimate that 45 million Americans would eventually develop cancer. "This means that malignant disease will strike two out of three families … *Today, more American schoolchildren die of cancer than from any other disease* [her italics]."

Carson herself was suffering from advanced breast cancer as she wrote the book, although she kept this information private. She believed her condition had been misdiagnosed (she had been told it was not malignant—it was common practice not to tell female cancer patients the truth). This only aggravated her mistrust of medical authority.

"[T]his courageous woman who launched the environmental movement," says Julia Brody of the Silent Spring Institute *(see page 114)*, "was afraid for anyone to know that she had breast cancer. She wore a wig to hide the effects of treatment." So these chapters, which dwell unflinchingly on liver damage, skin tumors, and leukemia, are a remarkable testament to Carson's bravery and personal commitment.

Her statistics struck a raw nerve in her audience; even to mention cancer in the early 1960s was to break a social taboo. Yet in 1960, leukemia killed 12,290 U.S. citizens. There was compelling evidence that the death rate per 100,000 people had risen sharply since 1950. Carson drew heavily on the work of controversial hematologist Malcolm Hargraves of the Mayo Clinic, who drew a connection between leukemia and DDT and other pesticides, bringing the meaning of the research home by presenting case studies of everyday people.

> *What do these case histories show? One concerned a housewife who abhorred spiders. In mid-August she had gone into her basement with an aerosol spray containing DDT and petroleum distillate. She sprayed the entire basement thoroughly, under the stairs, in the fruit cupboards and in all the protected areas around ceiling and rafters. As she finished the spraying she began to feel quite ill, with nausea and extreme anxiety and nervousness. Within the next few days she felt better, however, and apparently not suspecting the cause of her difficulty, she repeated*

*the entire procedure in September, running through
two more cycles of spraying, falling ill, recovering
temporarily, spraying again. After the third use of the
aerosol new symptoms developed: fever, pains in the
joints and general malaise, acute phlebitis in one leg.
When examined by Dr. Hargraves she was found to
be suffering from acute leukemia. She died within
the following month.*

This careful mixture of chilling statistics, tragic case histories, clear scientific explanation, and Carson's conscious efforts to tap into public paranoia about radiation make these chapters on human health powerful contributors to the overall impact of *Silent Spring*.

The Other Road

Carson was well aware that her book must offer some positive solutions to mitigate the doomsday scenario of the "Fable for Tomorrow," the fate of songbirds and eagles, and the alarming rise in leukemia and other human diseases. "I'm convinced there is a psychological angle in all this," she wrote to her editor Paul Brooks in 1958.

*[P]eople, especially professional men, are
uncomfortable about coming out against something,
especially if they haven't absolute proof the
"something" is wrong, but only a good suspicion. So
they will go along with a program about which they
privately have acute misgivings. So I think it is most
important to build up the positive alternatives.*

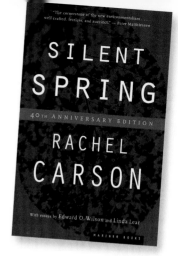

When her book came out four years later, her final chapter, "The Other Road" *(see pages 56–57)*, provided just such alternatives, before turning on the chemical industry one last time.

Carson was at pains to emphasize that she did not advocate the immediate or total abandonment of pesticide use, or even of aerial spraying. She recognized that "living in 'a sea of carcinogens' is of course dismaying and may easily lead to reactions of despair and defeatism." So what could be done? "It would be unrealistic to suppose that all chemical carcinogens can or will be eliminated from the modern world. But a very large proportion are by no means necessities of life." In addition to replacement and reduction, she urged greater research into alternatives. Carson continued to develop her ideas even after the book had gone to press. Her top priorities in the immediate aftermath of publication were the creation of a pesticide commission, in many ways presaging the Environmental Protection Agency, and the encouragement of grass-roots activism and citizen leadership, to offer a challenge, for example, to federal and state pest eradication programs.

Silent Spring started strongly. It led rapidly to five U.S. government inquiries into the impact of pesticides. A group of Carson's friends and fellow scientists met on June 25, 1964, at Rockefeller University's Scientist's Institute for Public Information. They agreed to set up the Rachel Carson Trust for the Living Environment (today known as the Rachel Carson Council) to investigate pesticide effects and alternative pest-control methods.

Fortieth-anniversary edition cover of *the* green manifesto. *Silent Spring* still sells strongly: more than 400 copies a week in the USA and UK, according to Nielsen BookScan.

The Other Road

We stand now where two roads diverge. But unlike the roads in Robert Frost's familiar poem, they are not equally fair. The road we have long been traveling is deceptively easy, a smooth superhighway on which we progress with great speed, but at its end lies disaster. The other fork of the road—the one "less traveled by"—offers our last, our only chance to reach a destination that assures the preservation of our earth.

The choice, after all, is ours to make. If, having endured much, we have at last asserted our "right to know," and if, knowing, we have concluded that we are being asked to take senseless and frightening risks, then we should no longer accept the counsel of those who tell us that we must fill our world with poisonous chemicals; we should look about and see what other course is open to us.

A truly extraordinary variety of alternatives to the chemical control of insects is available. Some are already in use and have achieved brilliant success. Others are in the stage of laboratory testing. Still others are little more than ideas in the minds of imaginative scientists, waiting for the opportunity to put them to the test. All have this in common: they are biological solutions, based on understanding of the living organisms they seek to control, and of the whole fabric of life to which these organisms belong....

Through all these new, imaginative, and creative approaches to the problem of sharing our earth with other creatures there runs a constant theme, the awareness that we are dealing with life—with living populations and all their pressures and counter-pressures, their surges and recessions. Only by taking account of such life forces and by cautiously seeking to guide them into channels favorable to ourselves can we hope to achieve a reasonable accommodation between the insect hordes and ourselves.

The current vogue for poisons has failed utterly to take into account these most fundamental considerations. As crude a weapon as the cave man's club, the chemical barrage has been hurled against the fabric of life—a fabric on the one hand delicate and destructible, on the other miraculously tough and resilient, and capable of striking back in unexpected ways. These extraordinary capacities of life have been ignored by the practitioners of chemical control who have brought to their task no "high-minded orientation," no humility before the vast forces with which they tamper.

The "control of nature" is a phrase conceived in arrogance, born of the Neanderthal age of biology and philosophy, when it was supposed that nature exists for the convenience of man. The concepts and practices of applied entomology for the most part date from that Stone Age of science. It is our alarming misfortune that so primitive a science has armed itself with the most modern and terrible weapons, and that in turning them against the insects it has also turned them against the Earth.

UNDERSTANDING RACHEL CARSON'S *SILENT SPRING*
IMMEDIATE IMPACT

Rachel Carson never expected to be lionized. She had already enjoyed massive sales for her book *The Sea Around Us*, but she knew that *Silent Spring* would be more challenging to a general audience, despite its impeccable timing, its readability, and her reputation. So she was delighted to be told, in the week before Christmas 1962, that from its publication in September the book had already sold 106,000 copies. This was astonishing for a book about pollution. *Publisher's Weekly*'s nonfiction best-seller list for 1962 shows that best sellers were meant to be about self-help, homemaking, sex—sometimes all three (*see box opposite*).

Strong sales continued in the first half of 1963, following the release of the paperback edition in January. As sales topped half a million, they reached a "tipping point" where everyone seemed to be reading the book, not just among the East Coast intelligentsia but on farms and in living rooms across the country and abroad. Even Snoopy and the gang, in the *Peanuts* cartoon strip drawn by best-selling cartoonist Charles M. Schulz, were talking about *Silent Spring*—in a 1963 strip, Linus complains that Lucy is always talking about Rachel Carson. "We girls need our heroes," she responds.

The book appealed particularly to young readers, giving these rebels a cause. "I can remember having these terrible arguments with my parents about spraying for bugs in the house and blanketing our lawns to keep them healthy and green with chemicals that I was sure were killing our dogs," explained the landscape photographer Robert Glenn

> *No wonder the impact of* Silent Spring *has been compared to that of* Uncle Tom's Cabin. *Both rank among the rare books that have transformed our society.*
>
> Former Vice President
> Al Gore, 1994

Ketchum. "For me personally, *Silent Spring* had a profound impact," recalled Al Gore, former U.S. vice president and longtime environmental activist. "It was one of the books we read at home at my mother's insistence and then discussed around the dinner table. My sister and I didn't like every book that made it to that table, but our conversations about *Silent Spring* are a happy and vivid memory."

U.S. President John F. Kennedy and Soviet Premier Nikita Khrushchev both looked up from the Cuban Missile Crisis to pay attention to the issues highlighted in *Silent Spring*. Supreme Court Justice William O. Douglas and writer E.B. White both thought that *Silent Spring* was as important as *Uncle Tom's Cabin* (1850), Harriet Beecher Stowe's abolitionist novel that did much to advance the antislavery campaign in the nineteenth century.

Before the Ink Was Dry

This is not an easy book to tell people about. We are going to have to work up something of a crusade—on a local level—if we are to reach a really wide audience.

Paul Brooks, editor, Houghton Mifflin, 1961

The *Silent Spring* team—Carson herself, editor Paul Brooks, agent Marie Rodell, and *New Yorker* editor William Shawn— were under no illusions as to the difficulty of promoting *Silent Spring*. Carson's own ambivalence about courting the media was one challenge—she was actually planning to be out of reach in Maine when the first installment appeared.

Publisher's Weekly nonfiction best-seller list 1962

1. Calories Don't Count, *Dr. Herman Taller (Simon & Schuster)*

2. The New English Bible: The New Testament *(Oxford University Press)*

3. Better Homes and Gardens Cook Book: New Edition *(Meredith)*

4. O Ye Jigs and Juleps!, *Virginia Cary Hudson (MacFadden-Bartell)*

5. Happiness Is a Warm Puppy, *Charles M. Schulz (Topper Books)*

6. The Joy of Cooking: New Edition, *Irma S. Rombauer and Marion Rombauer Becker (Bobbs-Merrill)*

7. My Life in Court, *Louis Nizer (Doubleday & Company, Inc.)*

8. The Rothschilds, *Frederic Morton (Atheneum)*

9. Sex and the Single Girl, *Helen Gurley Brown (B. Geis Associates/ Random House)*

10. Travels with Charley, *John Steinbeck (Viking Press)*

On the other hand, news of Carson's book had already reached top government echelons. In mid-May 1962, Interior Secretary Stewart Udall invited Carson to the White House Conference on Conservation, a month ahead of publication of the first installment in *The New Yorker*. Many influential delegates—including Supreme Court Justice William O. Douglas and Sierra Club Director David Brower—had received advance copies of the book. Udall was wondering whether he could use the pesticides issue to increase his influence with Kennedy, at the expense of his rival, Secretary of Agriculture Orville Freeman; he assigned a senior staff member to liaise with Carson. Congressman John V. Lindsay and Senator William Proxmire made overtures to Carson, raising the exciting prospect of legislation. Kennedy's special science adviser, Dr. Jerome B. Wiesner, convened an internal meeting of bureau chiefs to discuss Carson's articles, which set up a special interagency panel to report back to the president. On August 29, almost a month before *Silent Spring* was published, Kennedy referred to "Miss Carson's book" in a press conference.

Meanwhile, media interest also grew. CBS's popular news program, *CBS Reports,* was interested in doing a piece on *Silent Spring*. The consumer advocacy organization Consumer's Union offered to buy 40,000 copies for resale to members. The Book of the Month Club selected *Silent Spring* for its October choice. One chemical company—Velsicol—was less enthusiastic. Velsicol's legal counsel suggested that

The control room at Monsanto's Luling, Louisiana, plant in 1960. Monsanto reacted critically to *Silent Spring*, publishing a parody called "Desolate Year*"* warning what might happen if pesticides were banned.

Carson was part of a Communist plot to disrupt U.S. food supplies and threatened legal action against the book. All of this took place *before* the official publication date of September 27, 1962.

Men in White Coats: The Chemists Counterattack

Writing *Silent Spring* was a brave act. Although Senator Joe McCarthy's power had waned since the height of the anti-Communist witch hunts in the mid-1950s, anti-establishment thinking was still risky. Back in 1956, folk singer (and environmental campaigner) Pete Seeger was indicted for contempt of Congress by the House of Representatives, alongside playwright Arthur Miller and six others, after he refused to name names to the House Un-American Activities Committee (HUAC). It was 1961 when his case finally came to court, and Seeger was found guilty of contempt and sentenced to ten years in prison. (He was released the following year, when his case was dismissed on a technicality.) Although calmer minds were prevailing, conservatism still ruled.

> *We must at all costs avoid giving anyone the opportunity to yell "crank."*
>
> Marie Rodell,
> Carson's agent, 1960

At the same time, the chemical industry represented progress, a dominant theme of American life since the end of World War II. From the 1950s, America was determined to be prosperous and successful, and scientific advances were a major part of this. For example, Du Pont, like other chemical companies, had recently become a darling of the American consumer. It had invented nylon during the war,

The Du Pont pavilion, and behind it the Coca-Cola pavilion, were part of the 1964 World's Fair in Queens, New York. Chemical companies such as Du Pont had created a string of innovations and were very popular with ordinary Americans at the time.

and in 1962 it unveiled Lycra. In the 1960s it was advertising heavily to promise the housewife "Better things for better living ... through chemistry." Du Pont's "Wonderful World of Chemistry" pavilion at the 1964 World's Fair included upbeat song-and-dance presentations and exhibits such as the House of Good Taste. By daring to criticize the chemical companies, Carson was calling all of this into question.

Today's readers, accustomed to anti-corporate campaigners naming names, may be surprised by the scarcity of direct allegations of wrongdoing in *Silent Spring*. The late 1950s and early 1960s were a period of transition, when broad critiques of capitalist society were becoming more acceptable. *One-Dimensional Man* (1964) by political theorist Herbert Marcuse found a ready audience, as did *The Technological Society*, by French sociologist and theologian Jacques Ellul, which appeared in English translation the same year as *Silent Spring*. But specific criticisms of corporate America could be professionally risky. Vance Packard was denounced as a morality huckster and pop conspiracy theorist by the advertising industry when he named names in his best-selling *The Hidden Persuaders* (1957), criticisms that he never entirely shook off. William Longgood's *The Poisons in Your Food* (1960) was harshly dismissed by the chemical industry as being inaccurate (though Longgood later won the 1963 Pulitzer Prize for his journalism).

Carson was acting cautiously—very ill with cancer, money conscious, and with extensive family responsibilities, she meticulously avoided any mention of companies and brands. She was frightened not so much by the potential challenge to her reputation as by the real likelihood of financially crippling libel actions from the increasingly brand-conscious and litigious chemical companies.

She also feared that corporations would play dirty. Such fears were not misplaced. In 1965, a year after her death, Ralph Nader wrote *Unsafe at Any Speed*, attacking the safety of the General Motors Corvair. In response "GM hired private detectives to tail Nader in an attempt to dig up information that might discredit him," according to David Bollier, his biographer and an activist focusing on citizen action and public policy. GM "even had women accost him in an apparent seduction/blackmail scheme."

As it was, the chemical industry responded to *Silent Spring* with great indignation—Carson was accused of being a Communist and peace-nut. Pesticide manufacturers quickly mounted an attempt to discredit *Silent Spring* and its author, eventually spending at least $250,000 ($1.4 million in today's money) on refuting the charges levied in *Silent Spring*. In light of the fact that the wholesale pesticide market was worth some $1.65 billion, and that many of these companies had brand-new public relations departments, this is not in itself surprising. What is more surprising is that the media strategy almost seemed calculated to reinforce the

Rachel Carson is shown here at her typewriter in 1963. By nature shy and retiring, she reluctantly learned the value of media exposure to drive home her message on pesticides and ecology.

"Neanderthal" image, to use Carson's own description of the industry, that had so alienated environmental activists and their supporters.

Monsanto published and distributed 5,000 copies of a brochure parodying *Silent Spring.* Entitled "The Desolate Year," it envisaged devastation in a world in which famine, disease, and insects ran amok because chemical pesticides had been banned. Said one Monsanto man, "This was, for us, an opportunity to wield our public relations power."

"The Desolate Year" attempts to mimic Carson's writing style:

> *Quietly, then, the desolate year began. Not many people seemed aware of the danger. After all, in the winter, hardly a housefly was about. What could a few bugs do, here and there? How could the good life depend upon something so seemingly trivial as a bug spray? Where were the bugs anyway? The bugs were everywhere. Unseen. Unheard. Unbelievably universal.*

The National Pest Control Association penned a derogatory song called "Rachel, Rachel," and the National Agricultural Chemicals Association, the industry body leading the counterattack, brought out a more prosaic booklet called *Fact and Fancy,* attempting to refute excerpts of the book.

Other attacks, not only from the industry but also from politicians and the media, were more personal, questioning Carson's intellect, her integrity, and even her sanity. *Time* magazine criticized her "emotional and inaccurate outburst"; others called her "reckless," "a writer

WALDEN;
OR,
LIFE IN THE WOODS.
BY HENRY D. THOREAU,
AUTHOR OF "A WEEK ON THE CONCORD AND MERRIMACK RIVERS."

BOSTON:
TICKNOR AND FIELDS.
M DCCC LIV.

who has ventured into an unknown field," "more poisonous than the pesticides she condemned," and "baloney." "I thought she was a spinster," said a senior board member of the Federal Pest Control Review Board. "What's she so worried about genetics for?" Former Agriculture Secretary Ezra Taft Benson thought she was "probably a Communist." Not all attacks were based on knowledge of the book's content: As a report in the Bethlehem Pennsylvania *Globe-Times* said, "No one in either county farm office who was talked to today had read the book, but all disapproved of it heartily."

The government joined in the backlash. "The balance of nature is a wonderful thing for people who sit back and write books or want to go out to Walden Pond and live as Thoreau did," opined Ernest G. Moore of the Agricultural Research Service. But, he continued in a belated appeal to ordinary consumers, "I don't know of a housewife today who will buy the type of wormy apples we had before pesticides."

The counterattack spread quickly during what the *New York Times* called the "Noisy Summer" of 1962, following the June serialization in *The New Yorker* but before the book was published in September. Dr. Robert White-Stevens of American Cyanamid and former colleague-turned-academic Tom Jukes emerged as chief industry spokesmen. Both were intelligent and respected scientists. Even better, White-Stevens had an aristocratic-sounding name, an authoritative English accent, and a patrician manner. He was just what was

Critics wrongly accused Carson of being a latter-day Henry David Thoreau, with an elitist back-to-nature message. In fact, *Silent Spring* appealed to the preoccupations of ordinary suburban Americans.

needed—or so the industry thought. White-Stevens made dozens of attacks on Carson and the book, calling her "a fanatic defender of the cult of the balance of nature."

White-Stevens believed that

The crux, the fulcrum over which the argument chiefly rests, is that Miss Carson maintains that the balance of nature is a major force in the survival of man, whereas the modern chemist, the modern biologist and scientist, believes that man is steadily controlling nature.

Carson was too ill to be drawn fully into the battle, which may ultimately have worked to her credit. National Audubon Society's Roland Clement willingly took on the role of supporting the *Silent Spring* argument in frequent public debates. He soon found out that White-Stevens was a formidable intellectual adversary. Clement also learned that some members of the industry were not above General Motors-style dirty tricks. A team followed his every move on the lecture circuit. He became increasingly concerned for his safety when he managed to get hold of an unpleasant personal dossier about himself.

Roland C. Clement at the National Audubon Society in the late 1950s. With his tireless battles against industry spokesmen on the lecture circuit, Clement did more than anyone to spread the message of *Silent Spring.*

Throughout these concerted public relations campaigns, business continued as usual inside the chemical companies, and *Silent Spring* had relatively little impact on the research chemists themselves. Gideon D. Hill, Du Pont scientist in charge of urea herbicides in the 1950s, told Carson's biographer, Linda Lear, in an interview that Du Pont scientists failed to take much interest in *Silent Spring*, and that it did not demonstrably change their research priorities. The greatest phase of research and development in the company on pesticides came after 1962, but this was less a result of the *Silent Spring* agenda than of burgeoning opportunity. Lear concludes that although Du Pont's public relations department was acutely aware of the importance of the book and the lack of impressive response from the chemical industry, scientists themselves "were nearly oblivious to the public debate."

Letters to editors of periodicals from women across America suggest that the counterattack strategy pursued by the chemicals industry was counterproductive, winning publicity and support for the environmentalists. Carson was nevertheless hurt by the criticisms, especially the ones that denigrated her status as a scientist. Through the fall of 1962, Carson used her speaking engagements to respond forcefully to her critics, although she now was suffering from angina as well as cancer. Houghton Mifflin issued an advertisement and then a pamphlet in her support, highlighting the links between scientists and the chemical industry. An in-depth review in *Scientific American* was broadly supportive. But nothing the *Silent Spring* team did in their defense had as much impact as the chemical industry's decision to field the patriarchal White-Stevens alongside petite Carson on *CBS Reports*.

Television has pride of place in the living room of Mr. and Mrs. Franklin Streetcar in 1960s rural Massachusetts. Carson had little idea how influential the medium was to become, but made a star appearance on CBS in 1963.

Read It on TV:
15 Million New Readers in an Hour

When the message of *Silent Spring* moved from the soapbox to the living room box, a single hour on television did more to spread the message than its *New Yorker* serialization, bookstore sales, Book of the Month Club choice, and industry pamphleteering. In the early 1960s the power of TV to make or break a story was not widely recognized. But the enforced intimacy of TV, revealing public figures in a very different light, had already made, and broken, public figures—most notably a charismatic JFK and a sallow, sweaty Nixon in their first TV debate. Carson herself was no TV addict, had only recently bought a set, and worried that *CBS Reports* would show her in a bad light.

She was right to be concerned, because the show seemed weighted against her. Producer Jay McMullen and presenter Eric Sevareid had taken eight months to put the show together—a luxury that is unimaginable today. In addition to White-Stevens, they had interviewed a half-dozen senior members of government likely to be critical of Carson but few supporters. Shortly before the show went on the air, they received a thousand letters from an industry-organized letter-writing campaign, and three of the five corporate sponsors of the show pulled out because of the controversy. Finally, Gordon Cooper, on board the space capsule *Faith 7,* went into orbit as the program went out in May 1963, and live updates constantly interrupted the program (but also boosted viewing figures).

Carson need not have worried. On television, White-Stevens appeared overbearing rather than authoritative. "If man were to faithfully follow the teachings of Miss Carson," he boomed, "we would return to the Dark Ages, and the insects and diseases and vermin would once again inherit the Earth." Carson, by contrast, was measured, polite, concerned. The government interviewees did worst of all, revealing themselves to be ill informed, unconcerned, and evasive. Carson had the last word: "I think we're challenged, as mankind has never been challenged before, to prove our maturity and our mastery not of nature but of ourselves."

An estimated 10–15 million people watched the broadcast, compared with book sales of around half a million. Carson and CBS received hundreds of supportive letters; government officials got angry ones. The very next day, Senator Abraham Ribicoff of Connecticut began setting up a congressional committee to investigate pesticides, under the Senate Government Operations Committee.

Grand Central Station is filled to bursting as the crowd watches Gordon Cooper go into orbit, May 1963. TV coverage of the launch helped attract millions of viewers to a *CBS Reports* show on pesticides.

Silent Spring on the Hill

Although pollution control was no vote winner, it was definitely on the electoral agenda. "Conservation"—the precursor of environmentalism—had been mentioned during the 1960 Democratic and

> *Evidence continues to accumulate that she is right and that* Silent Spring *is the "Rights of Man" of this generation.*
>
> Brooks Atkinson, *New York Times*, April 1963

John F. Kennedy relaxes with paper and cigar. The president prided himself on being well read. One of his favorite magazines was *The New Yorker*, in which *Silent Spring* was serialized in 1962.

Republican conventions, and Carson had helped draft environmental policy for the Democrats. John F. Kennedy was interested in environmental issues (incidentally, William O. Douglas—surely the greenest Supreme Court Justice in U.S. history—was friendly with Kennedy as well as with Carson). JFK was a regular reader of *The New Yorker* and probably came across the *Silent Spring* story for himself. In a special message to Congress on natural resources in February 1961, he warned that lack of consistency and coordination of leadership meant that "one agency [was] encouraging chemical pesticides that may harm songbirds and game birds whose preservation is encouraged by another agency."

Even so, it is remarkable that, in mid-1962, despite being embroiled in the Cold War, the president found the time to ask the President's Science Advisory Committee (PSAC) to examine the use of pesticides and report back to him. Carson had an opportunity to get her view across at one of the famous Kennedy seminars, although she was eclipsed by the first rumblings of the Cuban Missile Crisis. She met informally with the PSAC and heard that JFK "often asked about the progress of the committee and urged speed in getting out the report." The pace was gathering. By the end of 1962, state legislators had already introduced 40 bills to regulate one or another aspect of pesticide use.

Carson, the environmentalists, and the chemicals industry anxiously awaited the release of the PSAC report in May 1963. In the event, Carson was delighted with the report and felt vindicated. It was critical of both the industry and government pest-control programs and called for steady reductions of persistent pesticides, although it did not specify how pesticides were to be regulated more effectively. The report also admitted that "until the publication of *Silent Spring*, people were generally unaware of the toxicity of pesticides." Carson was by then the focus of a follow-up report by CBS and on *The Today Show*. A second round of press coverage gave the issue yet more prominence.

Testifying in front of the Ribicoff Committee, Carson used the opportunity to set out policy options and to seek sponsors on the Hill to continue the momentum. In her 40 minutes before the Ribicoff Committee, she argued for the need to control aerial spraying and to reduce and then eliminate the most persistent pesticides. She demonstrated the need for a new bureau or commission to take responsibility for the testing of pesticides and the control of programs. She also spoke of citizens' right to be secure in their own homes against poisoning, seeing the need for some form of citizens' advisory committee to enforce this right.

Committee members—particularly Ribicoff—were impressed with Carson's integrity. But she understood only too well the world of "pork barrel politics," where government supports certain industries with special favors. In a speech to the Garden Club of America, she referred to the fact that tax deduction for lobbying expenses "means, to cite a specific example, that the chemical industry may now

work at bargain rates to thwart future attempts at regulation … The industry wishing to pursue its course without legal restraint is now actually subsidized in its efforts."

Carson's standing on the Hill was boosted by prestigious speaking engagements and a string of awards: the Cullem Medal from the American Geographical Society, the Paul Bartsch Award, and the Audubon Medal, culminating, in December 1963, with induction into the American Academy of Arts and Letters.

Once again, and for the last time, *Silent Spring*'s momentum was boosted by coincidence. Probably every American alive at the time can remember what he or she was doing on November 22, 1963, the day JFK was assassinated. But four days earlier, another dramatic killing had taken place on the banks of the lower Mississippi River. Carson had written in *Silent Spring* about the deaths of "hundreds or thousands of fish," and in 1960 there had been at least 30 large fish kills in Louisiana alone. But this time, 5 million fish died, including many catfish, a dietary staple in the bayous.

Journalist Frank Graham's 1970 book, *Since Silent Spring,* tells a classic detective tale, detailing how the culprit was revealed. Young public health officer Donald

Mount, using the latest gadgets and with help from industry insiders from Shell Chemical Company, first identified the pesticide endrin. But with more than 100,000 factories on the Mississippi, where had it come from? Following the trail upstream through the storm drains, the public health team eventually isolated a Memphis plant owned by Velsicol, the very company that had tried to shut down Houghton Mifflin with a legal challenge.

Extensive press coverage of the event only reinforced the message of *Silent Spring*. Weeks before Carson's death from cancer in 1964, the full story came out and public health officials grudgingly admitted that "Rachel Carson looks good." But Velsicol remained unapologetic: "In case you hadn't noticed," the company later announced, "trees leafed, birds sang, squirrels reconnoitered, fish leaped—1965 was a normal spring, not the 'silent type' of the late Miss Carson's nightmares."

> *Never doubt that a small group of thoughtful, committed citizens can change the world; indeed, it is the only thing that ever has.*
>
> Margaret Mead, anthropologist, in *Culture and Commitment: A Study of the Generation Gap,* 1970

Falling Silent:
The Untimely Death of Rachel Carson

Rachel Carson endured numerous rounds of radiation therapy for her breast cancer, which caused her pain and anguish not least because she feared a world made radioactive, contaminated by a nuclear bomb. Her medical misdiagnosis (she had been told her cancer was not malignant) and aggressive treatment did nothing to diminish her mistrust of the medical profession and the

Consumer advocate Ralph Nader appears before the press in 1979. General Motors used fair means and foul to discredit his first book *Unsafe at Any Speed* (1965), but Nader chalked up one success after another.

scientific establishment in general. On April 14, 1964—less than two years after the publication of *Silent Spring*—she died, exhausted by the long battle with metastatic cancer. Even close friends were amazed at how she had managed to keep the disease so secret.

"If only I could have reached this point ten years ago," Carson wrote in 1963. In fact, if *Silent Spring* had appeared in 1953, it would have sunk without a trace. But what might have happened if she had lived ten years longer? Might she have done as consumer advocate Ralph Nader did, following up on the success of *Unsafe at Any Speed* (1965) by producing one exposé after another, setting up a welter of public interest groups, and eventually running for president?

"Both books aggregated a lot of obscure and dispersed knowledge about their respective topics," says Nader biographer and policy expert David Bollier. "[They] galvanized a political response through their popularly accessible, lucid writing; provided a platform for their authors to become personified champions of an elusive set of issues having little cultural recognition; and helped define the movements that grew from the books." But even if Carson had been in good health, she was twice Nader's age when her book came out, and as she said to a friend, "One crusading book in a lifetime is enough."

Or could Carson have been another Betty Friedan *(see page 104)*, taking her best seller and forging a new activist movement through the judicious formation of a new

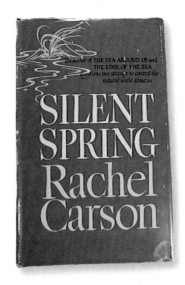

Silent Spring as it appeared on the bookstands in 1962. Rachel Carson was already well-known as the best-selling writer of books on marine biology.

national organization, calling upon women to strive for progress in environmental protection issues? The two women had much in common. Carson was becoming increasingly radical from the late 1950s on, and especially after *Silent Spring* was published. Although she did not see herself as a feminist, her attacks on the war against nature were by the end also attacks on the male establishment waging it. On the other hand, there was a reticence and pragmatism about Carson that would have made her uncomfortable as a radical campaigner.

It is impossible to say which direction Carson might have gone in if she had lived longer. What is certain is that by the time of Carson's death, her book had been read by more than 1 million people. Among them were a number of talented individuals ready to take on the challenges inherent in *Silent Spring*.

You've got to keep the opposition off-balance. Once you get them tumbling, you can't let up....

Ralph Nader to David Bollier, 1991

UNDERSTANDING RACHEL CARSON'S *SILENT SPRING*
LEGACY:
1964–1972

In 1958, six years before Rachel Carson's death, the Sierra Club's 15,000 members had failed to prevent reconstruction of the Tioga Road through Yosemite's Tenaya Lake area. Not a single fledgling robin was to be found on the Michigan State University campus, and only one young eagle was seen at Hawk Mountain. Fishermen struggled to find young salmon on the Miramichi River in New Brunswick, Canada. The outlook for North America's environment looked bleak.

> The legal victories won in the late sixties and early seventies formed the foundation on which the modern environmental movement is built.
>
> John Adams, founder, Natural Resources Defense Council, in *Crossroads: Environmental Priorities for the Future*, 1988

The eight heady years after Carson's death mark the birth of the modern environmental movement, blending wilderness conservation, pollution control, and human health. The movement gained an international perspective that had previously been lacking. In 1970, just six years after Carson died, 20 million Americans celebrated Earth Day. At the same time, the Clean Air Act was introduced, the Environmental Protection Agency was founded, and by 1972, the United States, along with many other countries, had banned the use of DDT.

But in all the green euphoria, material consumption grew unabated, along with the use of pesticides that made plentiful food and immaculate homes possible. Other toxic chemicals started to make their way into the marine and terrestrial environments, and persistent pollutants even reached the upper atmosphere. In 1972, few could have imagined that the ten-year-old *Silent Spring* would survive to have a midlife crisis.

DDT Through the Courts

Kennedy's assassination in November 1963 and Carson's death six months later put *Silent Spring* in limbo. The pesticides issue was no longer at the forefront—instead 1963 saw the Nuclear Test Ban Treaty and 1964 the Civil Rights Act. Although the chemicals industry was no longer allowed the automatic, and time-wasting, right to appeal against USDA bans, Congress had thrown out a bill allowing inspection of pesticide plants. Sales of still-registered products were growing fast—up by 10 percent in 1965 and 18 percent in 1966, reaching a retail value of $1.2 billion (more than $6 billion at today's value). In California's San Joaquin Valley alone, 500 pesticide salesmen had $25 million to use on promotions. President Lyndon B. Johnson's Science Advisory Committee, asked how to restore the quality of the environment, reported in 1965 that "The corporations' convenience has been allowed to rule national policy." Congressman Jamie Whitten enjoyed success with his engagingly written *That We May Live* (1966), with its blatant support for the pesticide industry.

Meanwhile, half a million American troops were heading for Vietnam. They were accompanied by Agents Blue, White, and Orange, powerful cocktails of herbicides used through the 1960s to deprive the enemy of forest cover and crops. Despite the innocuous names on the color-coded barrels in which they were shipped, these herbicides proved to be highly toxic—but not before 19 million pounds (8,618,255 kg) had been sprayed over the Vietnamese

Kennedy prepares to sign the partial Nuclear Test Ban Treaty with the Soviet Union in 1963. *Silent Spring* played on public fears by repeatedly likening pesticide pollution to radioactive fallout.

countryside and over tens of thousands of soldiers and Vietnamese citizens. The "war on nature" continued at home, too, involving sales of 80 million "bug bombs" (insect spray canisters) for hygiene-obsessed homes each year. By 1968, 1 billion pounds (453,592,370 kg) of DDT had been released into the environment.

No wonder Long Islander Carol Yannacone felt helpless when DDT spraying by the Suffolk County Mosquito Control Commission caused a fish kill in her favorite childhood haunt, Yaphank Lake. Unlike many of the housewives in *Silent Spring*, though, Carol's husband, Victor, was a young and aggressive lawyer. In 1966, he filed suit against Suffolk County, having teamed up with the Brookhaven Town Natural Resources Committee, an informal group of naturalists concerned about the loss of birds, butterflies, and crabs (from 1967, the group was known as the Environmental Defense Fund). The group was inspired by *Silent Spring* and its call for citizen action on pesticides—as well as by the earlier Long Island suit *(see page 33)* that had galvanized Carson in the first place.

Like Carson, the group stressed its scientific credentials. With experts such as Art Cooley, Brookhaven naturalist Dennis Puleston, Michigan ornithologist Lewis Batts, and marine ecologist Dr. Charles F. Wurster on board, Yannacone was convinced that he could win and had no interest in settling out of court.

Justice Jack Stanislaw had to look the word *ecology* up in a dictionary, but when Puleston showed him a series of watercolor paintings demonstrating the effects of DDT,

The Arctic was a pristine environment in the 1950s. By the late 1960s, though, persistent pollutants, including DDT, were regularly being discovered throughout the food chain— and in human inhabitants.

he exclaimed, "So that's why there are no more crabs in Great South Bay!" Nonetheless, the court ruled against the suit, but the Suffolk County Legislature had been sufficiently impressed by the evidence to order a halt to DDT spraying anyway. Although the EDF lost its first legal battle, it had won the war.

The EDF continued to put pressure on local governments. According to founding member Dr. Charles F. Wurster, it "was born from the frustration of a group of environmentalists unable to move the system, to make it respond, to force environmental protection." With crucial support from the Ford Foundation and National Audubon's Rachel Carson Memorial Fund, the EDF brought case after case against DDT and other pesticides. In Michigan, for example, it succeeded in getting 50 out of 57 municipalities to use pest-control methods less harmful to wildlife. In April 1969, Michigan was the first state to outlaw sales of DDT within state boundaries, spurred on by public outrage at the death of 700,000 Coho salmon fry in a local river.

In the meantime, research into DDT continued. British scientist Derek Ratcliffe was the first to discover the precise reason why DDT was a problem for birds such as bald eagles, ospreys, and peregrine falcons: It caused their eggshells to become excessively thin. His findings were soon matched at Patuxent Wildlife Research Center in Laurel, Maryland. DDT by this time had also been found in Antarctic penguins. It was soon detected in Arctic air, soil, snow, and ice, and virtually all levels of the Arctic food chain. Swedish

Surplus airplanes after World War II made aerial spraying a popular way to apply pesticides to crops and forests in massive quantities—but the impact on human bystanders and wildlife led to early protests against government pest control.

scientist Sören Jensen also unexpectedly found industrial fluids called PCBs (polychlorinated biphenyls) contaminating Baltic fish. These discoveries struck a nerve among naturalists, who had imagined that remote environments would remain pristine. Closer to home, the 1969 oil spills that blackened the beaches in Santa Barbara, California, also fanned the environmental groundswell.

In 1969, *Chemical Week* wrote an obituary for DDT, whose

> *marketing problems began in earnest with the publication of the late Rachel Carson's* Silent Spring. *Evidence: in 1957 the U.S. Department of Agriculture sprayed 4.9 million acres [19,380 sq km] with the pesticide; in 1967, [the] USDA sprayed only 100,000 acres [405 sq km] with it. Last year the figure was zero.*

However, reports of DDT's death were much exaggerated, or at least premature. After the EDF's successes on Long Island and in Michigan, said Dennis Puleston later, "Appeals for our aid in fighting environmental threats were pouring in." When the EDF responded by initiating lawsuits in Wisconsin and elsewhere, it found that the industry had assembled a task force on DDT, comprising all the main producers: Allied Chemical, Diamond Shamrock, Olin Mattiesen, Lebanon, and Montrose Chemical Corporation. Said Puleston, "The big chemical industry fought tenaciously to stop the bans."

There is still a debate about whether the industry was acting corruptly in its counterattack. Journalist Frank Graham in *Since Silent Spring* (1970) wrote of "pork barrel pesticides" and unfair government favors to the industry. Academic Robert Van Den Bosch wrote of *The Pesticide Conspiracy* (1978), and in *Hard Tomatoes, Hard Times* (1972) Jim Hightower wrote damningly of the vested interests of "the chemical boys." Hightower has continued to expose many problems resulting from what he sees as an industry-agricultural college-government coalition. Professor Tom Dunlap of Texas A&M University, who has studied the DDT story in detail, disagrees. "You should never attribute to malice what can be explained by incompetence," he says. The long-established triumvirate of industry, agricultural colleges, and government were, according to Dunlap's analysis, "honestly convinced they were doing wonderful things" in promoting agricultural productivity through mechanization and chemical applications. And in *Encounters with the Archdruid* (1971) Pulitzer Prize-winning writer John McPhee has written eloquently of the genuine differences in world view between an ecologist, the maverick David Brower *(see page 60)*, and three businessmen and engineers. In McPhee's book, Brower is painted as the "archdruid" because resort developer Charles Fraser fears conservationists as conspiratorial "religious figures who sacrifice people and worship trees."

The industry task force, headed by Louis A. McLean of Velsicol, offered a defense of DDT that proved to be both malicious *and* incompetent. The chemical press attacked the EDF directly, publishing the names and addresses of the EDF's board of trustees so that they could be targeted by

> We are losing half
> the subject matter
> of English poetry.
>
> Aldous Huxley to Julian
> Huxley, 1963

pro-chemical activists, and questioning its tax-exempt status. McLean accused the campaigners, in the journal *Bioscience,* of being "preoccupied with the subject of sexual potency to such an extent that sex is never a subject of jest," as though pesticide pollution and sterility were best treated in a lighthearted fashion. But the dirty tricks and snide comments backfired; such tactics were no match for carefully assembled documentation about wildlife damage, public fear over the possible health effects, and the evident failure of the spraying programs on their own terms as insect resistance grew. The anti-DDT movement was becoming unstoppable.

Litigation began in earnest as a result of the EDF's success. In 1970, naturalist John Adams established the Natural Resources Defense Council; it had a staff of professional lawyers (its current executive director, Frances Beinecke, ranks *Silent Spring* with *Sand County Almanac* as one of her most influential books). The Sierra Club set up a Legal Defense Fund. The National Wildlife Federation and National Audubon Society both started going to court, too. From 1968 to 1971, DDT use was soon outlawed, except under emergency conditions, in Illinois, Iowa, Massachusetts, New Mexico, New York, Rhode Island, Vermont, and Wisconsin.

The environmentalists did not rely solely on legal tactics. A new spirit of activism, learned from the civil rights and women's movements, inspired protests against dams, nuclear power plants, and highway projects, in addition to aerial spraying. They also launched press campaigns of their own. When levels of DDT were found in human breast milk that were seven times higher than that permitted in cow's milk, the EDF placed advertisements in the *New York Times* asking, "Is Mother's Milk Fit For Human Consumption?" DDT's invasion of breast milk made real the connection between humans and their natural environments.

Pesticide Control in Europe and Beyond

Silent Spring was published in all the Scandinavian countries in 1963. As early as 1969, when it became widely known in Sweden that DDT had been found in human breast milk, the Swedish promptly banned it (along with lindane, another toxic pesticide) for domestic use and also put a two-year ban on its field use. Denmark soon had a permanent ban on DDT. This was not an obsession of wealthy dairy-farming nations: Eastern bloc Hungary went further and banned *all* chlorinated hydrocarbon pesticides.

A heavy London smog, November 1953. Smogs killed thousands of Londoners in the early 1950s, and several hundreds in 1962, leading to pioneering legislation on clean air—and a British public sensitive to the issues raised by *Silent Spring.*

The largest wreath at Carson's funeral was from the United Kingdom's Prince Philip—an indication of the impact her work had in Britain. The publisher Hamish Hamilton issued *Silent Spring* in Britain in early 1963, with an introduction by Lord Shackleton and a preface by Julian Huxley, who later said, "The situation in Britain at that time was as grave as in the United States." The book was quick to prompt discussion at the highest levels. *Silent Spring* and its author were mentioned 23 times in a House of Lords debate in spring 1963. "I well remember watching from the public gallery," said naturalist Peter Scott, "and seeing two red spots below—the dust jackets of the English edition of *Silent Spring* beside the dispatch box on each side—one for reference by the government spokesman, Lord Hailsham, the other by the opposition spokesman, Lord Shackleton."

Londoners had suffered from notorious "pea-souper" smogs since the fourteenth century, when the first efforts were made to control coal-burning in the capital. In the 1850s, the stench from the polluted River Thames was so great that Parliament had to be suspended. The worst smog ever, in 1952, was responsible for thousands of premature deaths among the elderly.

These traumatic events set in motion the passage of the 1956 Clean Air Act—during a year when pigeons were seen falling dead from the sky—and diminished any British enthusiasm for the use of pesticides. There were no massive pest-control programs that required aerial spraying. But ornithologists soon suspected that practices such as the dressing of wheat seeds in highly toxic dieldrin, and the use of organophosphate pesticides such as sheep dips, had caused serious declines in bird numbers, including peregrine falcons, golden eagles, and songbirds. Particularly vexing for the hunting-shooting-fishing aristocracy was the loss of thousands of game birds such as pheasants.

The British response to these problems was pragmatic: voluntary restrictions on the most destructive uses and a voluntary testing regimen. One government official said, "It's really an organized muddle," but by 1966, most field uses of toxic pesticides aldrin, dieldrin, and heptachlor had ceased. Remarkably, it was the chemical industry itself that lobbied for more regulation. "We would like the voluntary scheme mandatory," said the Association of British Manufacturers of Agricultural Chemicals, "because it would absolve us of responsibility."

Academic Brigitte Nerlich, of the University of Nottingham, England, has carefully studied the power of the *Silent Spring* metaphor in the United Kingdom. "Over four decades the book *Silent Spring* has permeated public consciousness," she concluded. "The image of a 'Silent Spring,' which its title conjures up, has been used repeatedly as a rhetorical resource in debates about the impact of science on society and on the environment."

Other European countries were equally receptive to *Silent Spring*. "The hurricane you unchained is now over us," scientist C. J. Briejèr wrote Carson from the Netherlands in 1963. He went on to publish *Zilveren Sluiers en Verborgen Gevaren* (Silvery Veils and Hidden Dangers) in 1967. Authoritative but not compelling, and with a limited Dutch audience, it never achieved the sales of *Silent Spring*. In the same year, a French edition of *Silent Spring* was finally published, and by 1970 most countries across Europe were moving against pesticides.

Rachel Carson Silent Spring

The British edition of *Silent Spring* was highly influential, leading to long debates in Parliament and voluntary bans on pesticides. The book still sells strongly in the United Kingdom (140,000 copies since 1985). It now joined the ranks of Penguin Classics.

Pesticide problems spread far beyond Europe in the late 1960s. In the early morning of June 3, 1967, 500 people flooded into the sleepy government hospital in Qatar in the Persian Gulf. All had eaten bread for breakfast from the same baker. Seven people died. Exactly a month later, another 200 people were hospitalized, with 17 dead, before the culprit was finally tracked down. Wheat shipped from Houston, Texas, had been contaminated en route by leaky drums of highly toxic endrin. In September of that year, 17 children died in Tijuana, Mexico, from eating contaminated pastries. In November, parathion-drenched bread killed 80 people in Chiquinquira, Colombia.

[Earth Day] forged traditional conservationists into a union with newer constituencies worried about urban and industrial issues, thus giving birth to the modern environmental movement.

Dennis Hayes,
Earth Day organizer

The most tragic event, however, occurred in the village of San Joaquin, Bolivia. In 1965, 300 people died from a completely unexpected outbreak of black typhus. Health experts gradually pieced together what had happened. The typhus was carried by a small rodent called a *laucha*. Laucha had been rare in the village because these rodents were eaten by cats—until all the cats started dying mysteriously. One dead cat, which had been kept in a deep freeze, was sent to the United States for analysis by none other than Wayland Hayes, Carson's least favorite scientist. Hayes found the cat to be contaminated by DDT. The pesticide, widely used for pest control, had disrupted the web of life and led to the kind of human tragedy that Rachel Carson had envisioned.

By 1969, news of numerous wildlife and human health problems was coming from less developed countries. Public protest back in the United States was growing over the prodigal use of defoliant herbicides in Vietnam. The teach-ins of the anti-Vietnam protests also inspired planning for an unprecedented expression of public concern about the environment.

Environmentalism for All: From Earth Day to EPA

Former U.S. Senator and Wisconsin Governor Gaylord Nelson galvanized widespread support for the first Earth Day in 1970, a phenomenon comparable to Woodstock. Across the country some 20 million people took part in activities and events to raise environmental awareness. "A chorus of concern for the environment is sweeping the country," the President's Council on Environmental Quality wrote that year. "It reaches to the regional, national, and international environmental problems. It embraces pollution of the Earth's air and water, noise and waste, and the threatened disappearance of whole species of plant and animal life."

Above left: **A brown pelican comes in to land. Friends of the Earth founder David Brower credited Rachel Carson with helping to protect the species, and in 1973, The Endangered Species Act was passed.**

Above right: **Earth Day in Union Square Park, New York, April 22, 1970.** *Silent Spring* **called for citizen action on pollution, but its author would have been amazed by the sheer numbers of people who turned out.**

This chorus also encompassed popular culture: John Denver's third album included "Whose Garden Was This?," the first green pop song. (Admittedly, the album sold fewer copies than any record Denver had previously produced.) Novels, too, received a boost from Earth Day, notably Edward Abbey's popular *Monkey Wrench Gang* (1975). Membership levels in environmental groups increased as ecology moved toward the mainstream. In 1960 the Sierra Club had 16,000 members. It doubled in size to 33,000 by 1965, and had 114,000 members by Earth Day in 1970. Other established groups enjoyed similar growth. New groups also formed, notably Friends of the Earth—a new home for maverick ecologist David Brower *(see page 60)* when he was ousted from the Sierra Club after decades.

Jim Bohlen, John Cormack, Erving Stowe, and Paul Cote pose in front of the rusty fishing boat in Vancouver, British Columbia, 1961. Their plan to sail into the epicenter of a nuclear test explosion was the birth of Greenpeace.

Carson had known Brower quite well. Shortly before she died, they had visited Rodeo Lagoon and were treated to the sight of brown pelicans. "It was the first time I had seen them there," Brower recollected later. "Not surprising, given what DDT had previously done to their eggs. But there they were, thanks to Miss Carson and her book—a whole gaggle of brown pelicans, some two hundred of them, jubilant. So was she."

The environmental groups, whether old and establishment or new and brash, increasingly set their sights on targets other than conservation and the effects of pesticides on wildlife. New issues included childhood lead poisoning,

"Green" senators Edmund Muskie and Warren Magnuson show off electric scooters in Washington, D.C. Environmental policy made more rapid progress than electric vehicles in the 1970s as Nixon tried to outflank green opponents such as Muskie.

caused by lead in gasoline. The lobbying in Washington increased, with the Sierra Club being particularly vociferous. Russell Train, chairman of the Council on Environmental Quality in the Nixon administration, said, "Thank God for Dave Brower; he makes it so easy for the rest of us to be reasonable."

Amid all the legislation, the launch in September 1971 of *Greenpeace*, a filthy 80-foot (24 m) fishing boat attempting to bring about the end of atomic testing, went almost unnoticed. This was a mission Carson would have applauded but for which she would not have volunteered—she was no mariner. *Greenpeace* was soon a household word, with a brash but photogenic "actions speak louder than words" philosophy and Canadian Dave McTaggart firmly at the helm.

Unlike JFK, Nixon regarded the environmental movement as a dangerous fad run by antiwar radicals. Yet in 1969, he pushed through the National Environmental Policy Act, making it federal policy "to create and maintain conditions under which man and nature can exist in productive harmony." In 1970, Reorganization Plan No. 3 created the Environmental Protection Agency (EPA), ostensibly for administrative streamlining. But Nixon knew that this environmental record would take the wind out of the sails of "green" Senator Edmund Muskie, a potential rival in the 1972 presidential race. Given the importance of the economy to his reelection bid, Nixon tried to ensure that the EPA would not be able to jeopardize economic growth. But the EPA nevertheless did make sense, uniting a dozen functions from four branches of government described as "piecemeal" by Nixon in his special message of July 9, 1970: pesticide registration from the USDA; pesticide research and water quality from Interior; radiation and systems research from the Executive Office; and pesticide tolerances and air, water, and solid waste from Health, Education, and Welfare.

Banning the Bug Bomb

Despite the administration's hostility, the environmental movement scored its greatest successes during Nixon's presidency. Green politicians such as Gaylord Nelson and Edmund Muskie maintained the political momentum, helped along by litigation and media campaigning from the new environmental groups, and some saber-rattling exposés from "Nader's raiders"—notably John C. Esposito's *The Vanishing Air* (1970) and *Water Wasteland* (1971) by David Zwick with Marcy Benstock.

The new EPA, under William Ruckelshaus, was initially uncertain of itself, answerable both to the White House and to Congress, and looking only for easy victories that would cause little upset. But as the agency started to flex its muscles, a remarkable period of legislation followed, in which the new and stronger Clean Air Act of 1970 and the Clean Water Act of 1972 were highlights. The EPA found its role as a "gorilla in the closet," on hand for cities and states to use to frighten polluters into submission. It referred more than 150 cases of pollution to the Department of Justice in its first year.

In January 1971 the EPA spotlight turned controversially to DDT, and Ruckelshaus spent two months reviewing the case for a nationwide ban. Influenced by EPA experts who had been transferred directly from the USDA (nicknamed the "Department of Agribusiness" by Ralph Nader), and impressed by evidence prepared by the industry and agricultural colleges and presented in Congress by powerful friends such as Congressman Jamie L. Whitten (D-Mississippi), he was not convinced of the need for an immediate ban. Ruckelshaus ruled that DDT did not constitute an imminent health threat.

Carson had already cast doubts on the partnership between pesticide makers and universities. "The major chemical companies are pouring money into the universities," she wrote, "to support research on insecticides.... This situation explains the otherwise mystifying fact that certain outstanding entomologists are among the leading advocates of chemical control. Inquiry into the background of some of these men reveals that their entire research program is supported by the chemical industry.... Can we then expect them to bite the hand that literally feeds them?" Agricultural extension services, responsible for diffusing research innovations through to farmers, were also beholden to their clients. As journalist Frank Graham wrote in *Since Silent Spring* (1970), "USDA men in the field are not likely to say to their farmer-friends, 'Well, boys, it turns out I've been giving you bum dope for the last ten years!'"

The environmentalists whipped up popular protest against the industry case and forced the EPA to reconsider its decision. Throughout the spring of 1972, Ruckelshaus sifted through 9,000 pages of conflicting evidence from hundreds of experts. The effects on wildlife were furiously disputed, with scientists from the major companies picking through the data on bird toxicity to highlight puzzling exceptions. But Ruckelshaus was influenced by reports from two official commissions that pointed out DDT's persistent dangers to ecosystems and crucially suggested that DDT could pose a carcinogenic risk to humans.

The scientific debate was also being overtaken by local events. Under popular pressure, New York had banned DDT in parks, and other cities and states were also joining in with local bans. DDT wasn't working as well, either. Some 150 insect species were showing resistance to the pesticide, and more effective and lucrative products, such as carbaryl, were coming onto the market.

On June 14, 1972, ten years after *Silent Spring* had started appearing in *The New Yorker*, Ruckelshaus took a deep breath and announced a ban on virtually all domestic uses of DDT, exempting only a few emergency disease and pest-control applications. "Though unpopular among certain segments of EPA's constituency," writes EPA historian Dennis Williams, "his decision did serve to enhance the activist image he sought to create for the agency, and without prohibitive political cost." By late 1972, environmental progress seemed possible on all fronts. In ten years, *Silent Spring* had helped to eradicate the

JFK (center right) poses with his cabinet at the White House, 1961. Stewart Udall (Interior) and Abraham Ribicoff (Health, Education, and Welfare) were much more receptive to *Silent Spring* than Orville Freeman (Agriculture).

"perfect pesticide" and put a whole industry on the defensive, not just in the United States but in Europe and beyond.

In his book *Giant Killers* (1986), Michael Pertshuck describes five essential components of successful citizen lobbying campaigns. First, they need a broad "outside" grassroots movement or an organized constituency. Second, they need "inside" leadership within the executive branch, Senate, and House. Third, giant killers (those who campaign against the giants of industry) need a network of supportive policy experts. Fourth, they rely on an alert and sympathetic media. And fifth, they need professional, sophisticated lobbyists.

Silent Spring tapped into *two* broad grassroots movements: nature enthusiasts alarmed at wildlife losses, and suburbanites emerging from Cold War lethargy to worries about fallout, thalidomide, and cancer. The book found a devoted network of insiders such as Douglas, Ribicoff, Muskie, Udall … and JFK. Carson herself built up a loyal network of research and policy professionals across government departments and internationally.

Although the media as a whole was far from sympathetic, it was alert. *Silent Spring* would not have succeeded without *The New Yorker* and CBS. Finally, early advocates such as Roland Clement at Audubon were later joined by the savvy of the Environmental Defense Fund and the muscle of the Sierra Club to form a ten-year lobbying effort. In short, *Silent Spring* had all five components for an effective citizens' campaign.

UNDERSTANDING
RACHEL CARSON'S *SILENT SPRING*
AFTERMATH

Since the 1960s, popular culture—movies, TV, sculpture, painting, music, and photography—has helped galvanize public support for the environment. Multimedia web sites and mobile texting are the latest tools in green campaigning. Is there still a role for the crusading book? Although dozens of books have been heralded as "the new *Silent Spring*," none has had anything like its impact. In the 1980s and 1990s the phrases "acid rain," "nuclear winter," and "ozone hole" joined "silent spring" as defining environmental phrases, terms popularized by the media at large rather than by a single manifesto. These problems are now being addressed, in the same limited way that chemical pesticides have been dealt with.

Today, environmentalists warn of new, more difficult challenges—loss of biodiversity, endocrine disruption, genetic modification, and global warming. These issues still lack a defining image. No single text has emerged to grab American readers wherever they are—in the White House, the town house, or the little house on the prairie. Without such public support, it is harder to motivate official and concerted action to address these newly identified threats.

Today, the environmental groups that were fledgling in Carson's day have at least 9 million U.S. members (the Sierra Club alone claims 700,000). Some groups are even considered "mainstream" in their desire to work with industry and government to create lasting change rather than end-of-pipe solutions. Yet the spirit of radical protest is still alive and well, as the 1999 protests in Seattle against the World Trade Organization and the huge popularity of American campaigner and filmmaker Michael Moore's documentaries show. Earth First! and hundreds of local activist groups reject efforts to work with a global system that they see as fundamentally flawed. Despite some mutual antagonism, the two strands of environmentalism operate a reasonably effective "good cop/bad cop" routine.

Environmental politics have also come a long way since John F. Kennedy and Richard Nixon ate potentially contaminated cranberries *(see pages 34–35)* and Nixon sent the IRS out against the Sierra Club. Carson would have been encouraged by the environmental credentials of presidential hopefuls such as Al Gore and Howard Dean, and by the existence of strong green lobbies in Congress—but dismayed by the waves of environmental deregulation under the administrations of Ronald Reagan, George H.W. Bush, and George W. Bush.

Silent Spring's long-term effect is hard to fathom. It is undoubtedly the most influential environmental book ever. Yet more pesticides are used, more money is made from pesticides, and more people die from pesticide poisoning today than when it was written. The book is accused of having caused millions of deaths from malaria by journalist Steven Milloy, and there are vociferous advocates for DDT's continued use around the world.

Two environmentalists from Earth First! take "direct action" by placing a banner on the Lincoln Memorial in Washington, D.C., in 1987. Deforestation in the United States and tropics aroused widespread protests by "tree huggers" in the 1980s and 1990s.

This chapter is *not* a canned environmental history since 1972. It looks briefly at the growing scale and complexity of environmental and human health challenges and asks, what concrete impact—if any—did *Silent Spring* really have on the issues that followed in its wake?

The Impact on the Pesticides Industry and Farming

> It is ... *reassuring to note the progress that can be made in science and technology, once clear national goals are established. The success of Apollo 11 in placing men on the moon is a dramatic case in point. The current public interest in pesticide pollution offers promise for significant advances in our knowledge through research.*
>
> National Academy of Sciences, 1970

Faith in progress through science and technology is one of the defining features of the 1960s. *Silent Spring* did not diminish the importance of scientific progress; rather it tried to promote accountability and responsible progress. Carson worked to put the science of ecology, and the ecological approach to nature, on the map and have it taken seriously by fellow scientists. Her critique of chemical pest control was proven to be largely correct, but her search to discover new methods was cut short by her death.

A key part of accountability is regulation, and the U.S. government has treated the pesticides industry with some ambivalence since *Silent Spring*. The search had been secretly on since 1963 for regulation that industry could live with. "If you want it banned," Senator Abraham Ribicoff told Roland Clement of the National Audubon Society during a coffee break at the 1963 hearings over DDT, "don't mention exports." After all, regulatory approval for the use of DDT applied only within the United

States, and losing this was not as great a loss as the industry pretended. Nearly 140 insect species were already resistant to it by 1962. More toxic but less persistent alternatives were under development or coming onto the market, many of which would be more profitable for the home market. And after the ban on its use, the half-dozen U.S. companies producing DDT still managed to keep producing DDT for export—a lucrative loophole. Throughout the 1970s, USAID (the U.S. Agency for International Development) actually specified the use of DDT in its programs. As late as 1990, the United States was still exporting $68 million of domestically banned, canceled, or restricted pesticides from total pesticide exports of around $500 million.

Rachel Carson was a meticulous science writer who feared being labeled a crank. Her critics used sexist comments to undermine *Silent Spring*, but could find very few errors.

There have been plenty of other domestic concessions to the industry since then. "For the most part, hardliners within the pesticide industry have succeeded in delaying the implementation of protective measures called for in *Silent Spring*," wrote Al Gore in his preface to the American 40th anniversary edition of *Silent Spring* in 1994. "It is astonishing to see the cosseting this industry has been accorded in Congress over the years."

At the same time, use of pesticides has increased. From 617 million pounds (279,866,492 kg) of "active ingredients" (the chemicals that do the actual killing) in the year of Carson's death, consumption in the United States rose steeply, almost doubling to its peak of 1.14 billion pounds (517,095,301 kg) in 1979. Since then, the total amount has declined slightly, to 912 million pounds

Top: **The destructive boll weevil is originally from Mexico. The weevil persists in Southern states despite decades of attempts to eradicate it. It causes millions of dollars of damage to cotton crops.**

Above: **Plant physiologist Chester McWhorter conducts trials on low-volume herbicide application methods. Despite such efforts, volumes of pesticides used in the United States remain far higher today than in 1962.**

(413,676,241 kg) in 1999, but this is still one-and-a-half times the amount used in 1964. Patterns of use have changed markedly. Herbicides have grown in importance, whereas insecticides now account for just 10 percent of the U.S. market. But the ongoing federal boll weevil eradication campaigns in cotton-growing states such as Texas and Oklahoma show that the aerial spraying of insecticides such as malathion remain crucial, alongside mapping and trapping pests. And different crops have shown different trends. The amount of active ingredients used on apples has halved, but the amount used on potatoes has skyrocketed.

The industry says it has worked hard to reduce the impact of pesticides while meeting demand and improving effectiveness in the face of growing insect resistance and inexorably rising world population. Certainly, crop losses to pests remain very substantial in the United States and around the world—estimates vary widely, from 12 percent to 40 percent of total production.

Pesticides have changed considerably since the days when DDT was sprayed from planes. They are more targeted and less persistent, many applied in just ounces per acre. Overall, *expenditure* on pesticides has gone up significantly. In other words, farmers and householders may be using smaller quantities of pesticides than at the peak, but today the pesticides are more powerful—and more costly. When the Environmental Working Group (EWG) analyzed more than 100,000 U.S. government pesticide test results, it found 192 different pesticides on 46 popular fresh fruits and vegetables. Nectarines were top of the list (97 percent of samples tested positive for pesticides), followed by pears and peaches (94 percent).

Rachel Carson clearly stated, "It is not my contention that chemical pesticides must never be used"—but she did believe they could be significantly reduced. Yet the world now spends $33.6 billion on pesticides, and that amount is climbing. The United States spends one-third of that—$11 billion a year. Three-quarters of American households still use pesticides. But surely pesticides are much safer since *Silent Spring*?

Not necessarily, warn the environmentalists. Environmental and human health problems, and ever-growing levels of resistance, continue to challenge the industry and its regulators. In 1982 groundwater contamination was first reported on Long Island, New York, from the pesticide aldicarb. In 1993 Cornell entomologist David Pimentel estimated that 67 million birds were still being killed each year by pesticides. In 1999—the latest year for which the EPA has data on use—9 million pounds (4,082,331 kg) of the organophosphate chlorpyrifos was still being used in insecticide products. Since then it has been banned because new regulations required a risk analysis of domestically used pesticides on infants and children. After three decades of use in homes, chlorpyrifos was found *not* to be safe.

So the criticisms Carson made about inadequate testing still ring true. Green groups accuse the industry of backsliding, and sometimes of duplicity. But as former Du Pont

A technician checks dishes containing tiny experimental peach and apple trees grown from laboratory-cultured cells with added genes. *Silent Spring* briefly warns of biotech developments, but Carson did not reveal her support for the organic alternative.

Chairman Charles McCoy once observed, "Private corporations live by public permit." The public, enraged as it was by *Silent Spring*, has continued to be seduced by an American dream of cheap food and bug-free homes. In a sense, as Carson put it, "The people [have] done it themselves."

Other pest control methods have failed to achieve sufficient support to sway the balance away from the use of pesticides. For example, the 1996 report (resulting from a United Nations Environment Program workshop in 1992) *Beyond Silent Spring*, by pest-control experts Helmut van Emden of the University of Reading and David Peakall of King's College, London, makes a strong case for "integrated pest management (IPM)." IPM is a judicious blend of nonpesticidal tactics such as biological predators and farm hygiene—and minimal, timely applications of chemicals only at the threshold at which crop losses become uneconomic. The authors of the report conceded that Carson was right "in many respects," but claim that "human life span is still increasing. Society has responded, and, of course, birds still sing." Carson would have approved. However, IPM has not made much of an impact because the U.S. food business now largely backs genetically modified organisms, and especially herbicide tolerance, as the key to pest control. "Some would-be architects of our future," wrote Carson, "look towards a time when it will be possible to alter the ... germ-plasm by design." If she'd lived, she would have seen it herself. The first gene-splicing took place in California in 1973.

Search the text for "chemical pesticides" and replace with "genetically modified organisms," and *Silent Spring* would offer a reasonably modern-sounding attack on today's food industry. The speed at which genetic modification has moved from theory through laboratory through half of all U.S. foodstuffs is similar to the DDT story. Many of the companies are the same, and behaving in familiar ways. As with the use of chemicals, the lack of information on the effects of genetically modified organisms (GMOs) on wildlife and human health has not stopped the industry from making broad claims of safety—and moral claims of necessity on behalf of the world's poor.

Best-selling writer Jeremy Rifkin warns of new technological dangers to society and the environment. Carson was an early supporter of organic farming and would likely have condemned genetic modification.

Biotechnology has some capable critics, none more so than the prolific writer Jeremy Rifkin, whose *The Biotech Century* (1998) is the most widely read book in the world on the social and environmental dangers of biotechnology. However, unlike the pesticide story, the vast majority of public outrage against genetic engineering has come from outside the United States, catching the U.S. proponents of biotechnology genuinely by surprise. They cannot have been reading their *Silent Spring*.

Many environmentalists argue that organic farming is the wave of the future, and its preference for natural pest-control methods over chemical ones means that it is more in keeping with the ethos of *Silent Spring*. They claim consumers are demanding more healthful—chemical-free and additive-free—choices in the supermarket. Europe is taking the lead in organic agriculture, increasingly cautious

Thanks to the Endangered Species Act (1973), this national emblem, a bald eagle, is present in the United States in healthy numbers once again. In 1962, it seemed more likely to disappear from the Lower 48 states.

after the devastation to the beef industry wrought by "mad cow disease" (bovine spongiform encephalopathy—BSE). In some countries, entire baby food product lines are now certified organic. But even in the United States, organic products are one of the fastest-growing segments of the food industry. Sales of organic products, according to Gary Hirshberg of the organic food company Stonyfield Farm, have grown at a rate of 22 percent annually for more than ten years. Today, the farming debate is increasingly polarized between the extremes of genetic modification and organic.

The Bald Eagle Flies Again: The Impact on Wildlife

Silent Spring saved the eagle. The DDT ban, coupled with private, state, and federal conservation efforts and the Endangered Species Act, has indisputably brought the bald eagle back from the edge of extinction. In 2000 there were nearly 6,500 pairs in the Lower 48 states, compared to just over 400 in the early 1960s. Twice as many eagles are regularly seen in the National Audubon Society's annual Christmas Bird Count as then. Other birds of prey, too, have recovered their numbers, although less dramatically.

The salmon was another lead character in *Silent Spring*, and the situation remains grim. In the early 1990s, Seattle citizens chose healthy salmon as a key indicator of the area's sustainability, because of their environmental, economic, cultural, and social importance. But in the first comprehensive survey since then, Washington State reported that just 40 percent of its wild stocks can be classified as healthy, down slightly from 1992. Salmon populations on the Miramichi River of New Brunswick *(see page 76)*, on Canada's Atlantic coast, are, however, in better shape.

Of all the wildlife in *Silent Spring*, the American robin is arguably the central character. Here, the news is mixed. Critics of Carson seized on a freak mass roosting in Nashville, Tennessee, in the early 1960s, which made robins seem incredibly abundant. Numbers seen since then in the Christmas Bird Count fluctuate from year to year but are not discernibly higher than they were in the 1960s. In the United States and Europe, populations of songbirds remain vulnerable to habitat loss, intensive agriculture, and pesticides. The British Trust for Ornithology's popular bird census shows a dramatic fall in the numbers of U.K. farmland birds such as the skylark and corn bunting since the 1960s. The trend was confirmed in a 1999 paper for *Nature* entitled "The second *Silent Spring*?"

Mammals are in general much safer from modern pesticides, but if birds, fish, and friendly insects are exposed before the pesticides lose their potency, the results can still be devastating. In addition, organophosphate pesticides are still widely used around the world. India and China still produce and use DDT and other rogue pesticides for agricultural purposes. In Mumbai (Bombay), traditional Parsee "sky burials" have been suspended because there are not enough buzzards left to do a thorough job of cleaning the corpses. In the winter of 1995–1996, 20,000

The robin is no longer dying by the dozen on America's "lethal lawns." Worldwide, however, many bird species are still threatened by harmful pesticides.

Bees remain vulnerable to many modern pesticides. "It is a very distressing thing," says a beekeeper in *Silent Spring*, "to walk into a yard in May and not hear a bee buzz."

Swainson's hawks died in Argentina after feeding on grasshoppers contaminated by pesticide. This was 5 percent of the world's entire population of this rare bird in one fell swoop. The pesticide was banned in 1999. In 2003 the French environmental group Robin des Bois accused Beaujolais Nouveau wineries of being a threat to the environment. "The Beaujolais (region) produces more polluted water than wine," they said, because of the huge amounts of pesticides used in wine making. Bees are particularly vulnerable to some new types of pesticide.

In general, *Silent Spring* did bring dramatic benefits for the web of life. DDT has been disappearing from ecosystems, although not as fast as was hoped. But certain types of wildlife still remain in peril from pesticides. The situation is serious in countries with weak pesticide controls—nowhere more so than in India and China, where DDT is still in legal use.

Love Canal and the Feminine Mystique

In 1963 Betty Friedan challenged the long-established paradigm—that women could find fulfillment only as wives and mothers—in her book, *The Feminine Mystique*. "I have just finished reading your splendid book and want to tell you how excited and delighted I am with it," early feminist trade union activist Gerda Lerner wrote Friedan in February 1963. "You have done for women what Rachel Carson did for birds and trees." Carson and Friedan both gave voices to ordinary housewives. Increasingly, women have been using that voice to challenge the chemical industry.

In 1952, at Love Canal, near Buffalo, New York, the Hooker Chemical Company sold a plot of land to the local school board for just $1 (and claimed a tax deduction for this "charitable" act). The only catch was that Hooker had previously dumped 21,000 tons of toxic waste chemicals on the site, which began to leak out and cause health problems for students and local residents almost as soon as the land was built on.

By 1977, local residents such as Lois Marie Gibbs were growing worried about risks of chemical exposure for their children. "I began going door to door with a petition to shut down the 99th Street School," recalls Gibbs. "It became apparent, after only a few blocks of door knocking, that the entire neighborhood was sick. Men, women, and children suffered from many conditions—cancer, miscarriages, stillbirths, birth defects, and urinary tract diseases." In August 1978, the New York State Department of Health finally declared a state of emergency at Love Canal, leading to the evacuation of 940 families. The cleanup effort has cost at least $250 million to date. Gibbs is now known as "The Mother of Superfund"—the federal fund for cleaning up contaminated sites.

Chemical waste dump. At least 20,000 contaminated sites have been identified in the United States since Love Canal provoked a national scandal in 1978. *Silent Spring* made what was at the time a controversial link between chemicals and cancer.

Erin Brockovich-Ellis provided another dramatic example of environmental activism. A file clerk at a Southern California law firm, she did some solo legal sleuthing in the mid-1990s and uncovered the fact that the health of hundreds of residents around the Pacific Gas and Electric Company Compressor Station in Hinkley had been devastated by toxic chromium-6 leaching into groundwater.

In 1996, as a result of the largest class action lawsuit of its kind, PG&E paid the largest court settlement for injuries caused by toxic chemicals in U.S. legal history. "If for one minute I had ever thought that this case was going to settle for $333 million and a movie starring Julia Roberts with a $2 million bonus," said Erin Brockovich-Ellis, "I think I would have been committed."

Carson never saw herself as an advocate on women's issues. Like Friedan, she was forced to abandon a PhD, and her freedom to write was limited by restrictive social mores and family expectations; she was also critical of the male scientific establishment. But she herself was far from being a trapped housewife and told *Life* magazine in 1962, "I'm not interested in things done by women or men, but in things done by people." In *Silent Spring* she was open to contributions from all kinds of sources, including the male science establishment. But by tapping into a world of housewives concerned by the changes they were noticing in the world around them, she identified an emerging trend.

Friedan was no more an ecologist than Carson was a feminist, but "ecofeminism" has been a driving force in local activism since the days of Love Canal. Public attitude surveys, in country after country, consistently find that women express more concern over the state of the environment than do men. They also favor more stringent environmental laws and more public spending for environmental protection than do men, according to Professor H. Patricia Hynes of Boston University's School of

Public Health. The ordinary housewives who first expressed their concerns in *Silent Spring* have become the eco-feminists driving local activism ever since.

Living Downstream: Act Local

By 1980, as many as 23,000 toxic dumps had been identified across the United States, and the EPA set up a "superfund" of $1.6 billion to help deal with them. The cleanup has been painstakingly slow, urged on by frequent litigation and gradual improvements in the public's right to know about toxic releases. But new toxic hot spots may be being generated faster than the old ones can be cleaned up.

Addressing this issue, Sandra Steingraber's *Living Downstream* (1997) has been heralded as a "new *Silent Spring*." Like its precursor, it is notable for its rigorous research, including its meticulous juxtaposing of toxic-release data and the recently available cancer registry data. Steingraber was in part motivated to write by the debate that occurred over the building of a waste incinerator in her own neighborhood, a small town near Peoria, Illinois—a debate that is a late-twentieth-century equivalent of the aerial spraying of pesticides. Instead of the anonymous town described in *Silent Spring*, Steingraber identifies real cancer hot spots throughout the nation. Her book is carefully and lyrically written, like Carson's. However, rather than simply presenting the facts, Steingraber gave her story a novel-like treatment. "Carson would have been scorned for writing the kind of book I did," says Steingraber. "I felt that I *had* to create

Sandra Steingraber's *Living Downstream* is a modern telling of the devastating experience of ordinary American women in the face of environmental pollution.

a powerful first-person narrative on which to hang the science ... just to keep my readers turning the pages." Carson put herself into her book just once: This was not to discuss her own cancer—unmentionable in literature at the time—but to reminisce about student days growing protozoa in a test tube.

Living Downstream makes an important contribution to the controversial debate on environmental cancer. Although the book never hit the best-seller lists, Steingraber—far more an activist than Carson ever was—made sure it got into the hands of health and environmental activists, where it has been influential. It is therefore surprising that the book has drawn only muted criticism. Skeptic Ron Bailey, science correspondent for *Reason* magazine, has written dismissively about "The Great Cancer Scare launched by Carson and perpetuated by her environmentalist disciples ever since," but fails to furnish compelling counterevidence. Perhaps because environmental cancer investigations implicate such a broad range of industry sectors, no one sector in particular has felt targeted and thus required to prepare a focused counterattack.

The Nature Conservancy designated some 50 islands and 11 coastal preserves in Maine as the Rachel Carson Seacoast. Her birthplace in Allegheny County, Pennsylvania, has not been so lucky. It is ranked among the United States' worst 10 percent of counties in terms of major chemical releases and waste generation, according to the scorecard compiled by a not-for-profit group, Environmental Defense, from the EPA's 2001 Toxic Release Inventory. (The

web-based scorecards are available for every county in the United States.) PPG Industries' complex in Springdale, Carson's birthplace, was alone responsible for pumping more than 250,000 pounds (113,398 kg) of toxic chemicals into the atmosphere in 2001. Forty years after *Silent Spring*, not enough is being done to minimize toxic releases. But at least communities have the right to know where the pollution comes from, which they did not in Carson's day.

Silent Spring raised consciousness of industrial pollution, but environmentalists are still fighting hard to reduce pollution. Toxic releases in Allegheny County, Pennsylvania, where Carson was born, actually increased significantly in the final decade of the twentieth century.

Our Stolen Future: Think Global

In 1968 *Apollo 8* took a portable television camera into space, beaming back images, to millions of rapt viewers, of the Earth as a small, delicate, blue globe suspended in the void. This image has had enormous influence on the development of a global environmental consciousness, as powerful in its way as the image of the nuclear mushroom cloud.

In a famous paper in *Science* in 1983, Carl Sagan and colleagues warned of the terrifying possibility of a "nuclear winter." But nuclear war is, of course, not the only global risk. In 1974, University of California chemists Sherwood Rowland and Mario Molina showed that protective ozone in the stratosphere could be destroyed by chlorofluorocarbons (CFCs). This academic paper found no Carson to popularize it. Quite the opposite: NASA satellites were specifically calibrated *not* to detect substantial ozone losses, so unlikely did they seem to most scientists. The ozone hole was finally spotted and publicized in 1985 by Joe Farman of the British Antarctic Survey. It took a further

15 years of vigorous campaigning and international negotiation through the Montreal Protocol, convened by the United National Environment Program in 1985–1987, to begin the long international process of agreeing to phase out the production of CFCs and other ozone destroyers.

A similar timescale elapsed between scientists' figuring out that acid rain was behind damage to forests and lakes and an international agreement about how to reduce it. The most dramatic response was in Germany, where the phenomenon of "forest death" in the early 1980s galvanized ecologists into forming the Green Party. With Petra Kelly, the Green Party went on to make significant inroads into mainstream politics, finally winning several cabinet posts in the 1998 coalition government. The German Green Party's successes have been copied but never fully replicated in other European countries. And although acid rain helped to introduce green politics, it never produced a memorable green manifesto.

Bill McKibben's *The End of Nature* (1989) is another possible contender as "the new *Silent Spring.*" McKibben's bleak but beautifully written book tackles global warming as a result of ever-growing emissions of carbon dioxide into the atmosphere. He argues that the scale of the climate disruption on its way means the end of the natural world as a phenomenon independent from human interference. The cultural, technical, and commercial changes needed for the United States to wake to global warming are enormous (although greater

This forest was devastated by acid rain, caused by industrial emissions of sulfur and nitrogen. In the 1970s and early 1980s, rain in the Great Lakes and Ohio River valley region was more acidic than root beer.

action in some European countries shows that they are not impossible). By contrast, he argues, dealing with DDT was pretty straightforward. But was it?

In the early 1970s, contaminants such as DDT and PCBs started showing up in the most remote places—on land, at sea, in animals such as the beluga whale and Antarctic penguin. Often called the "dirty dozen," these persistent organic pollutants (POPs) are found wherever someone looks for them. We carry in our bodies up to 500 synthesized chemicals that did not even exist in the 1920s. "We are accustomed to look for the gross and immediate effect and to ignore all else," warned Carson. "Unless this appears promptly and in such obvious form that it cannot be ignored, we deny the existence of hazard." She flagged the possibility that persistent chemicals could interfere with reproduction. Highly complex scientific evidence has been building in the past decade that POPs at very low levels can indeed subvert the operation of human and animal hormones, especially among infants and fetuses. This is known as endocrine disruption.

One recent book on the subject has won mass readership. *Our Stolen Future* (1996) by Theo Colborn, senior program scientist at the World Wildlife Fund, painstakingly amasses evidence about endocrine disruption, drawing on 4,000 scientific papers on subjects as disparate as the Great Lakes ecosystem and the human body. Carson worked on pesticides alone or with scientists one-on-one. In contrast, Colborn, the so-called "grandmother with a PhD in

Bill McKibben's best-selling book on global warming in an updated 2003 edition. McKibben also writes regularly for *The New Yorker*. Of Carson, he says: "She pointed out the problem; she offered a solution; the world changed course."

Theo Colborn, the "grandmother with a PhD in toxicology," co-authored *Our Stolen Future* to draw attention to the environmental causes of alarming reproductive and developmental problems in humans.

toxicology," organized a meeting for 100 scientists at the Wingspread Conference Center in Wisconsin in 1991 to make sense of endocrine disruption. Wingspread participants soon discovered a shared consensus that wildlife population crashes, preterm births, falling sperm counts, and—most controversially—lower IQ are among the many possible results of low-level contamination by persistent chemicals.

When the book appeared in 1996, it was hailed as "the new *Silent Spring*," and Colborn, the new Rachel Carson. Colborn vigorously disputes the comparison with Carson. For one thing, she had two co-authors—Dianne Dumanoski and John Peterson Myers—to help translate the scientific synthesis into understandable prose. For another, the team used focus groups, rather than a writer's instinct as Carson did, to discover how to get the unappealing message across to a broad public.

The book was attacked with familiar epithets such as "alarmist" and "speculative." Chief critic, endocrine expert Dr. Steve Safe of Texas A&M University, "has made some very derogatory remarks about the book," said Colborn to journalist Doug Hamilton in February 1998. "But he has also admitted he has never read it. And he doesn't intend to." In general, however, the industry response has been more "no comment" than "baloney." "I think in many instances they'd rather ignore me," says Colborn.

What has been the impact of *Our Stolen Future*? Well, there has been more research on the long-term toxicity of chemicals such as DDT, for one thing. Take the recent piece of detective work by Matthew Longnecker and colleagues at the National Institute of Environmental Health Sciences and the U.S. Centers for Disease Control. In 2001 they published their results in the prestigious British health journal *The Lancet*. Using new chemical techniques, they analyzed mothers' blood samples stored at babies' births during the 1950s and 1960s. What they found was dynamite: a very strong association between DDT levels and "an epidemic of pre-term birth." Another study has shown DDT to cause a decrease in the length of time that mothers breast-feed. In fact, Longnecker estimated in a controversial interview in the *New Scientist* that up to 15 percent of infant mortality in the United States during the years of heavy DDT use may have been attributable to the pesticide. If he is right, DDT *may* have been responsible for tens of thousands of infant deaths a year in the United States alone.

Victims of the explosion at Union Carbide's chemical plant in Bhopal, India, in December 1984. Methyl isocyanate gas killed 3,300 local people and injured 20,000 others. Along with Seveso (1976) and Chernobyl (1986), it was one of the world's worst industrial disasters.

Our Stolen Future has helped push along the U.N.'s Stockholm Convention to phase out all POPs, which has 151 countries on board. The convention entered into force when 50 countries ratified it. At the time of writing, 151 countries have signed the convention. The United States has not signed. Progress in efforts to control the manufacture and disposal of the most dangerous POPs was spurred by the industrial accident at Seveso, Italy: In July 1976 an explosion in a chemical plant released a cloud of dioxin (one of the most toxic man-made chemicals), which settled on local communities. The aftermath of the accident was seriously mishandled, but led to strong European legislation on industrial safety—as well as the assassination of one of the plant managers by terrorists. An even more tragic accident in Bhopal, India, in 1984 led to some improvements in industrial safety in the developing world.

Environmental campaigners today see the dirty dozen POPs as the tip of a toxic iceberg. Some 87,000 chemicals are in common use today, according to the Silent Spring Institute, a partnership of scientists, physicians, public health advocates, and community activists united around the goal of identifying and changing the links between the environment and women's health, especially breast cancer.

Most of these chemicals have not yet been tested for toxicity. This is not an academic issue. A 2003 survey of 120 homes in Cape Cod, Massachusetts, by five researchers for the Silent Spring Institute found an average of 45 hormone-disrupting chemicals in the home, not just in pesticides but also in detergents, plastics, and furniture, and in personal care products such as cosmetics and hair treatments. Basic information—let alone health-based exposure guidelines—is lacking for many of the compounds.

No wonder some environmental groups have grown frustrated by the slow case-by-case process. Citing the so-called "precautionary principle," they propose the phasing out of whole families of suspect compounds—including PVC (polyvinyl chloride). Greenpeace tried a decade ago with its "Chlorine-Free in 93" banner. The World Wildlife Fund (WWF) discovered in 2003 that 99 percent of a sample of people in the United Kingdom still have DDT-related chemicals in their bodies, 30 years after it was banned. Findings like these have caused WWF's Global Toxics Initiative to set itself the ambitious, but possible, target of ending threats to biological diversity from toxic industrial chemicals and pesticides—especially endocrine-disrupting, bioaccumulative, or persistent chemicals—within one generation, not later than 2020. The chemical industry is, not surprisingly, unenthusiastic.

The Malaria Minefield

Each year around the world, 1 million people are poisoned by pesticides, and some 20,000 die. Every 30 seconds an African child dies of malaria. Throughout the tropical and subtropical regions of the world, malaria causes more than 300 million acute illnesses and at least 1 million deaths annually. Both sets of numbers, from the mid-1990s, are from the World Health Organization, which has found itself caught in the crossfire in a controversy about the role of DDT in malaria control.

The malaria situation today is far worse than when Carson was writing. Malaria parasites have become resistant to one drug after another, and many insecticides are no longer useful against mosquitoes. Science still has no "magic bullet" for malaria, and many doubt that such a single solution will ever exist. The Roll Back Malaria global partnership, a WHO-led international partnership aiming to halve malaria by 2010, promotes a package including insecticide-treated nets and affordable antimalarial drugs for

DDT was effective in the fight against malaria, carried by mosquitoes, in the 1940s and 1950s. However, problems with mosquito resistance, more than *Silent Spring*'s campaign against pesticides, meant that it was gradually dropped in most countries.

Soft drinks are sold from a cart in Agra, India. In 2003, researchers revealed that domestically produced soft drinks, including Coca-Cola and Pepsi, contained unsafe levels of pesticides, including DDT. Parliament temporarily banned the drinks.

local treatment; together these can reduce transmission of the disease by as much as 60 percent and the overall young child death rate some 20 percent.

"No responsible person," says *Silent Spring*, "contends that insect-borne disease should be ignored." Lobby groups such as the Competitive Enterprise Institute and Africans Fighting Malaria, and even Harvard's Center for International Development, have been vociferous against the international DDT ban. According to Richard Tren, chairman of Africans Fighting Malaria, "The use of small amounts of DDT means the difference between life and death for thousands of people in the developing world every day."

After fierce international debate, DDT is now the one chemical for which exceptions are allowed in the Stockholm Convention. It can still be used in two dozen countries, including Ecuador, Madagascar, Ethiopia, and South Africa, until they can develop alternatives for mosquito control. Outside China, which still makes and uses DDT in unknown quantities, Hindustan Insecticides Ltd. of Kerala, India, is the last remaining known producer of DDT, with an annual production in the region of 10,000 tons a year for domestic consumption and export. Greenpeace investigated the wetland around the factory in 1999 and found it—not surprisingly—to be thoroughly contaminated.

Neither China nor India have supported the Stockholm Convention and, as "rogues," have used DDT as they like. In India, DDT is legally permitted only for mosquito control, but Indian farmers can readily get hold of it and of other banned products such as Aldrin. The result is that in addition to farmer poisonings and wildlife losses, DDT levels in mothers' milk are among the highest in the world. "This not only illustrates the loopholes in the pesticides legislation in the country," says Madhumita Datta, a campaigner for the Indian campaign group Toxics Link, "but also the apathy of enforcement agencies."

Public opinion, however, may finally be beginning to turn against persistent pesticides in India. In August 2003 the Delhi-based Centre for Science and Environment alleged that a dozen soft drink brands produced in India, including Coca-Cola and Pepsi, contained dangerously high levels of lindane, DDT, malathion, and chlorpyrifos. The accusation created uproar in Parliament and public protests involving smashing bottles on the streets—and prompt legal action from the manufacturers.

Whether or not to use DDT for mosquito control in countries such as India and South Africa will remain a controversial debate for years to come. This debate has even resurfaced in the United States. Steven Milloy, publisher of junkscience.com, is currently advocating the use of DDT to control West Nile Fever. Although he fails to address the tricky issue of insect resistance, the media loves a contrarian. The *New York Times* even ran an opinion piece calling for DDT use in the United States in August 2003— more than 40 years after Carson struck a seemingly mortal blow to the philosophy that "nothing must get in the way of the man with the spray gun."

UNDERSTANDING
RACHEL CARSON'S *SILENT SPRING*
CONCLUSION

> *Books do not have the same power to change the world that they once had. They occupy a different, more marginalized place in our culture now. I would bet that not even Hillary Clinton's new book has that kind of draw across the socio-economic spectrum. I don't think there can ever be another* Silent Spring.
>
> Sandra Steingraber

Silent Spring Is in the Air

Rachel Carson would have been delighted with *Silent Spring*'s continuing commercial success— 2 million copies by the book's 40th anniversary in 2002, and counting—and even more so by the critical acclaim from its immensely appreciative audience. She was fortunate to have enjoyed at least some of the fruits of her literary success before her death two years after publication.

Silent Spring exposed the hazards of pesticides such as DDT, about which the American public had been generally unaware. And despite the chemical industry's ill-advised public relations counterattack, Washington insiders knew that a ban on DDT was only a matter of time—and horse trading. In this way, *Silent Spring* contributed substantially to the regulation of those pesticides at home and abroad.

The bald eagle owes its life to *Silent Spring*, as do many other species and habitats. Millions of Americans and others around the world must also thank Rachel Carson for their health and their lives—just how many is still hotly disputed and will probably never be agreed on. But the lack of "bite" in regulations concerning toxic chemicals would have disappointed Carson. The United States today uses 50 percent more pesticide than it did in the year that she died. And the list of environmental and health problems that these pesticides cause is growing, not shrinking.

Regulating persistent pollutants has been difficult, as the stories of POPs, acid rain, the ozone hole, and toxic waste testify. Even those who believe the regulatory process is on the right track accept that it is slow and imperfect. Many others fear that risks expand faster than solutions—both in geographical scope and complexity. The recently identified phenomenon of endocrine disruption—seen from North Pole through South, and from beluga whales through 60-day-old human fetuses—is a compelling case for regulation.

Rachel Carson in 1952 was a best-selling but low-profile marine biologist. Over the next decade, she transformed herself into a manifesto writer with what she called her only "crusading book," *Silent Spring*.

Silent Spring is credited as being the mother—or at least the midwife—of the modern environmental movement. Certainly, in terms of the numbers involved, and the sophistication and diversity of approach, the movement is incomparable to the small, cliquey, conservation-dominated groups of the early 1960s. *Silent Spring* drew together the wildlife and human health movements, and Earth Day celebrated their union. The two movements have worked toward a common cause ever since—although it has not always been easy.

The book also provided a launching pad for environmental politics. Some were opportunistic, others idealistic. Ironically, a cynical opportunist such as Nixon has left greater monuments than many an idealist. Nevertheless, Carson would probably have been surprised at the spectacle, in the run-up to the 2000 presidential elections, of Al Gore and Ralph Nader fighting over their green credentials—a dramatic contrast to Kennedy and Nixon's cranberry-eating, contamination-denying exploits 40 years earlier.

Silent Spring can be read narrowly or widely. Narrowly, it is about DDT and other pesticides and the problems they cause wildlife and humans. Widely, it is a radical critique of humanity's blind faith in technological progress and the "control of nature"—and as such it has continued to be inspirational.

Carson increasingly believed that the male scientific psyche was to blame for the war on nature. This is an intriguing part of the book's legacy today. Although she did not invent ecofeminism, she certainly laid the foundations for a later generation. *Silent Spring* also cautiously probed the consumer culture for which America had just begun to develop a taste, without addressing it directly. The book made little dent in that appetite, which grows apace, fueling global warming as well as ongoing toxic pollution, and is the subject of many new crusading authors, such as Naomi Klein (*No Logo*, 2002) or Eric Schlosser (*Fast Food Nation*, 2002).

Carson also critiqued the "needless havoc" risked by scientific progress undertaken more for the challenge and profits than to meet any genuine need—this is the argument put forward today by opponents of the use of GMOs in industrial agriculture. *Silent Spring* shows pesticides to be not modern miracles but "as crude a weapon as the cave man's club." Some of the alternatives she proposed—such as the sterilization of male insects by irradiation—were constrained by the time in which she was living. In other ways, her solutions were ahead of her time.

Surely if *Silent Spring* was as powerful a manifesto as some enthusiasts declare, an irate public would by now have come to terms with global warming and genetic modification. Companies would be listening carefully, to try to learn the rules of the new game. Scientists would be working in a new, precautionary paradigm. And the government would be exerting moral leadership on the international stage. But this has just not happened. Does this mean that *Silent Spring* was ultimately a failure as a crusading manifesto?

Well, just how much can you ask of a book? The real testament to *Silent Spring* as a manifesto is that it is still inspiring activists and writers, entrepreneurs and policy makers today, nearly 50 years later. Some later books have effectively and bravely exposed the new threats to the environment and human health, sparking a new spirit of activism, although none has yet reached the mass audience that *Silent Spring* found. The town in the heart of America is still in trouble. Defending the web of life has turned out to be a far harder battle than anyone realized in 1962, but *Silent Spring* is still in the prime of life.

GLOSSARY

catalyst A person or thing acting as the stimulus in bringing about or hastening a result.

compound Made up of two or more separate parts or elements; a substance containing two or more elements chemically combined in fixed proportions and in which the constituent elements lose their individual characteristics while the resulting compound has new characteristics.

conservation The act of protecting something from loss or waste; the care and protection of natural resources.

consternation Great fear or shock leading to a sense of helplessness or bewilderment.

diversity Characterized by difference and variety.

ecology The branch of biology that concerns the relations between living organisms and their environment.

efficacy Power to produce the intended effects or results; effectiveness.

fungicide Substance that fills fungi or slows or halts the growth of spores.

innocuous Harmless.

insecticide Any substance used to kill insects.

interdependence Dependence on each other; mutual dependence.

lobby To try to get lawmakers to vote for or against a certain measure that affects a special interest that the one who is doing the lobbying represents.

manifesto A public declaration of motives and intentions by a government, group, or individual regarded as being of some importance or wielding some influence.

persistent Refusing to relent; stubborn; continuing to exist or endure; lasting without change.

pesticide Any chemical used for killing insects, weeds, and other unwanted pests who threaten crops, trees, plants, and other foliage.

preservation The act of saving something or protecting it from harm or loss.

synthesize The putting together of parts or elements to form a whole.

synthetic Produced by chemical synthesis, rather than of natural origin; artificial; not real or natural.

toxicity Characterized by being poisonous.

utilitarian Stressing usefulness over beauty or any other consideration.

UNDERSTANDING
RACHEL CARSON'S *SILENT SPRING*
FOR MORE INFORMATION

Environmental Defence Canada
317 Adelaide Street West
Suite 705
Toronto, ON M5V 1P9
Canada
(416) 323-9521
Web site: http://www.
    environmentaldefence.ca
This Canadian environmental
    organization promotes environmental
    protection.

Friends of the Earth
1717 Massachusetts Avenue,
Suite 600
Washington, DC 20036
(202) 783-7400
Web site: http://www.foe.org
Friends of the Earth and its network of
    grassroots groups in seventy-seven
    countries defend the environment and
    champion a more healthy and just
    world. Its current campaigns focus on
    clean energy and solutions to global
    warming, protecting people from toxic
    and new, potentially harmful
    technologies, and promoting smarter,
    low-pollution transportation
    alternatives.

Greenpeace
702 H Street NW
Washington, DC 20001
(202) 462-1177
Web site: http://www.greenpeace.org/usa
This global environmental organization has
    campaigned on environmental issues
    since 1971.

The Nature Conservancy
4245 North Fairfax Drive, Suite 100
Arlington, VA 22203-1606
(703) 841-5300
Web site: http://www.nature.org
The conservancy is a conservation
    organization with ongoing projects
    around the world aimed at protection
    of land and water. They identify
    principal threats to marine life,
    freshwater ecosystems, forests, and
    protected areas, then use a scientific
    approach to save them.

Rachel Carson Homestead
613 Marion Avenue, Box 46
Springdale, PA 15144
(724) 274-5459
Web site: http://www.rachelcarsonhomestead.
    org/Home/tabid/36/Default.aspx

The mission of the Rachel Carson Homestead Association is to preserve, restore, and interpret Rachel Carson's birthplace and childhood home and to design and implement education programs and resources in keeping with her environmental ethic.

The Sierra Club
National Headquarters
85 Second Street, 2nd Floor
San Francisco, CA 94105
(415) 977-5500

Web site: http://www.sierraclub.org
Founded in 1892, the Sierra Club is the United States' oldest environmental organization.

Web Sites

Due to the changing nature of Internet links, Rosen Publishing has developed an online list of Web sites related to the subject of this book. This site is updated regularly. Please use this link to access this list:

http://www.rosenlinks.com/wtcw/rcss

UNDERSTANDING RACHEL CARSON'S *SILENT SPRING*
FOR FURTHER READING

Beatty, Rita Gray (1973) *The DDT Myth: Triumph of the Amateurs*, John Day

Bollier, David (1989/91) *Citizen Action and Other Big Ideas, A History of Ralph*

Nader and the Modern Consumer Movement (available at www.nader.org)

Brooks, Paul (1983) *Speaking for Nature: How Literary Naturalists from Henry*

Thoreau to Rachel Carson Have Shaped America, Book Sales

Carson, Rachel (1941) *Under the Sea-Wind: A Naturalist's Picture of Ocean Life*, Simon & Schuster

Carson, Rachel (1951) *The Sea Around Us*, Oxford University Press

Carson, Rachel (1955) *The Edge of the Sea*, Houghton Mifflin

Carson, Rachel (1962) *Silent Spring*, Houghton Mifflin

Colborn, Theo, Dianne Dumanoski, and John Peterson Myers (1996) *Our Stolen Future*, Dutton

Curtis, Jennifer, and Lauri Mott (1993) *After Silent Spring: The Unsolved Problems of Pesticide Use in the United States*, Island Press

Dunlap, Thomas R. (1982) *DDT: Scientists, Citizens, and Public Policy*, Princeton University Press

Graham, Frank (1970) *Since Silent Spring*, Hamish Hamilton

Guerrero, Peter F. (1992) *Pesticides: Thirty Years Since Silent Spring*, Diane Publishing Co.

Hough, Peter (1998) *The Global Politics of Pesticides: Forging Consensus from Conflicting Interests*, Earthscan

Hynes, H. Patricia (1989) *Recurring Silent Spring*, Elsevier

Lear, Linda (1997) *Rachel Carson: Witness for Nature*, Henry Holt

Marco, Gino, Robert Hollinsworth, and William Durham (1987) *Silent Spring Revisited*, Washington, D.C.

Rudd, Robert (1964) *Pesticides and the Living Environment*, American Chemical Society

Steingraber, Sandra (1997) *Living Downstream: An Ecologist Looks at Cancer and the Environment*, Addison-Wesley

Taylor, Robert E. (1990) *Ahead of the Curve: Shaping New Solutions to Environmental Problems*, Potomac Publishing/ Environmental Defense Fund

Van Den Bosch, Robert (1978) *The Pesticide Conspiracy*, University of California Press

Waddell, Craig (ed.) (2000) *And No Birds Sing: Rhetorical Analyses of Rachel Carson's "Silent Spring,"* Southern Illinois University Press

Weir, David (1987) *The Bhopal Syndrome: Pesticides, Environment and Health*, University of California Press

White-Stevens, Robert (ed.) (1971–77) *Pesticides in the Environment*, Dekker

UNDERSTANDING
RACHEL CARSON'S *SILENT SPRING*
ABOUT THE AUTHOR

Alex MacGillivray researches and writes about environmental and social problems. He has worked with a wide range of environmental groups, including the World Wide Fund for Nature, Greenpeace, and Friends of the Earth, as well as advising government and business on sustainable development. Recent publications include *Communities Count* (1997), *Low Flying Heroes* (2000), and *Secrets of Their Success* (2002). Alex studied modern history at Oxford University and ecology at Imperial College, London. For ten years he worked for the New Economics Foundation, a London-based think tank.

He now lives in remote rural France with his wife and two daughters.